DEAD END

Gary E. Goldhammer

BIDDLE
PUBLISHING
COMPANY

PO Box 1305, Brunswick, Maine 04011

Publisher's Cataloging in Publication Data
1. Goldhammer, Gary E.
2. Dead End
3. Capital punishment
4. Death penalty
5. Death Row
6. Prisoner advocacy
7. Prisoners and prisons

Library of Congress Catalog Card No. 94-71783

ISBN 1-879418-15-0

This book is printed on recycled paper.

For my father

TABLE OF CONTENTS

"The death penalty is cruel and unusual because it is imposed infrequently and under no clear standards. Its purpose, whether retributive or deterrent, cannot be achieved when it is so rarely and unpredictably handed out."

—1972 United States Supreme
Court ruling, Furman vs. Georgia.

INTRODUCTION

"Everyone gather 'round, please."

Dale Riley, a spokesman for the Missouri Department of Corrections, was about to make an announcement. I picked up my notepad and joined the other journalists who, for the past several days, had called the dark, musty state penitentiary home.

"About 10 minutes ago, the Eighth Circuit Court of Appeals granted a stay of execution for Gerald Smith," he said in his good ol' boy monotone. "It's not gonna happen tonight."

The dejected pack of news hounds loaded up their cameras, microphones and portable computers and went outside. We walked past the band of candle-bearing death penalty opponents, whose once silent prayers had turned to jubilant celebration, drowning the cries of "kill the bastard" from capital punishment supporters standing nearby.

Another long night had come and gone, and as 1988 drew to a close, Missouri was still without its first execution in 23 years. Smith, convicted of beating his girlfriend to death with an iron bar, had canceled another performance. The faces of my fellow reporters told the story — weeks of hype and preparation, and again, no payoff.

But there would be other days. After another false start, Gerald Smith was finally executed. He wasn't the first person executed in the United States — and he would not be the last.

Just ask Doyle Williams, one of Smith's fellow inmates whose own execution date is fast approaching. Or ask Bob Doemer, who nearly was executed in Ohio for a crime he didn't commit. Ask Marie Deans, who fights against capital punishment despite her mother-in-law's murder; or Patti Linebaugh, who would like to see

Theodore Frank die in California's gas chamber for torturing and killing her two-year-old granddaughter.

Ask November West from Greenwich Village who is married to a man on Death Row in Texas; or Charlie Jones, the warden in Alabama who offers college courses and television sets to the condemned; or Joe Ingle, the Tennessee preacher nominated for the Nobel Peace Prize for his work to abolish the death penalty — and who stopped visiting inmates because their pain has become too much for him to bear.

Ask the prosecutor. Ask the defense attorney. Ask the people who cheer because they believe the death penalty is right — and ask those who cry because they believe capital punishment is wrong.

The specter of execution lives with them and it lives with us. No one is immune.

Unlike the wounds opened by the loss of a relative or a close friend, the wounds opened by the death penalty bleed with irony. Even with a bare-bones appeals process, it costs more to execute than to keep inmates in jail for the rest of their lives. Death Row inmates charged with one murder live just cell blocks away from lifers who have killed more people, more brutally. Inadequate legal counsel and overzealous prosecutors have put innocent people on Death Row — some are reprieved, for others it's too late. Black defendants whose victims were white are executed; white defendants whose victims were black rarely make it to Death Row.

Murderers must be punished, but that punishment should not compromise justice and decency. It should not belittle us or our humanity.

Whether brought about by nature or sanctioned by society, death makes all of us suffer — we cannot deny it or escape it. But capital punishment is real only because we have made it a reality. The death penalty doesn't have to exist. It doesn't, as shown by the fact that most countries don't have capital punishment, *need* to exist.

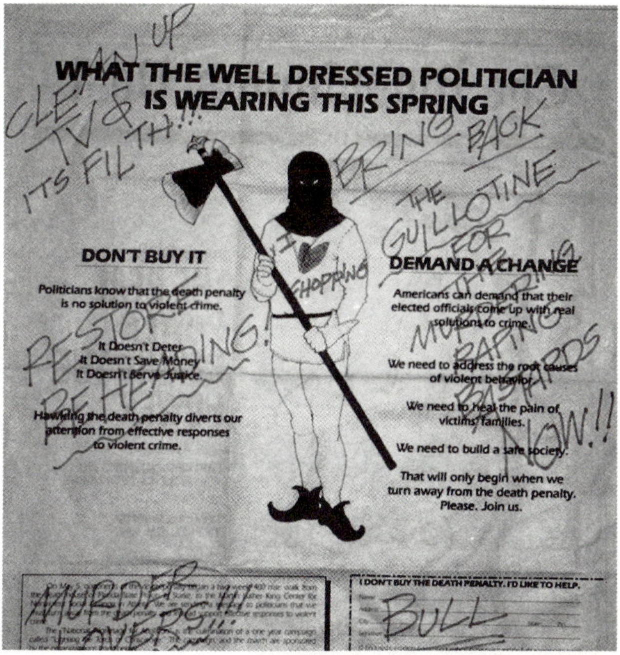
WHAT THE WELL DRESSED POLITICIAN
IS WEARING THIS SPRING
DON'T BUY IT
Politicians know that the death penalty is no solution to violent crime.
It Doesn't Deter
It Doesn't Save Money
It Doesn't Serve Justice.
Hawking the death penalty diverts our attention from effective responses to violent crime.
DEMAND A CHANGE
Americans can demand that their elected officials come up with real solutions to crime.
We need to address the root causes of violent behavior.
We need to heal the pain of victims' families.
We need to build a safe society.
That will only begin when we turn away from the death penalty. Please. Join us.
I DON'T BUY THE DEATH PENALTY. I'D LIKE TO HELP.
CLEAN UP TV & ITS FILTH!!
BRING BACK THE GUILLOTINE FOR MURDERING BABY RAPING BASTARDS NOW!!
RESTORE BEHEADING!
MURDER LOVERS!!
BULL

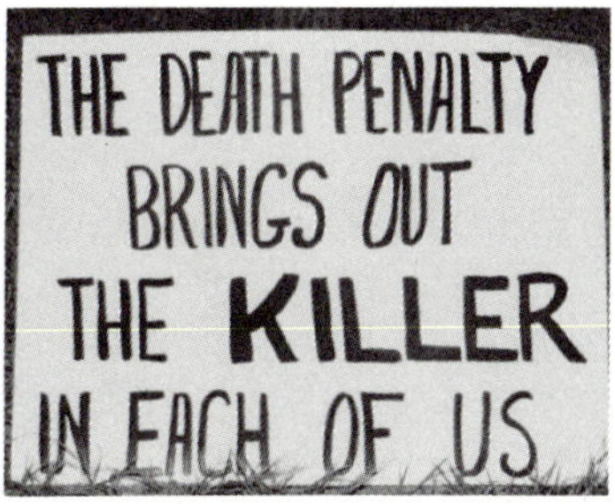
THE DEATH PENALTY
BRINGS OUT
THE KILLER
IN EACH OF US

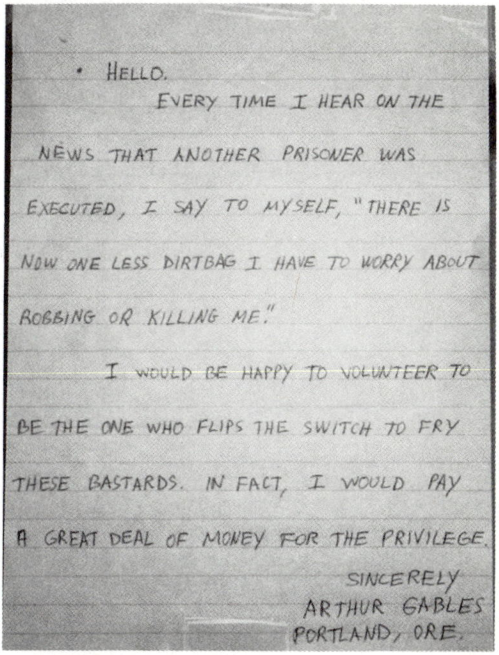
HELLO.

EVERY TIME I HEAR ON THE NEWS THAT ANOTHER PRISONER WAS EXECUTED, I SAY TO MYSELF, "THERE IS NOW ONE LESS DIRTBAG I HAVE TO WORRY ABOUT ROBBING OR KILLING ME."

I WOULD BE HAPPY TO VOLUNTEER TO BE THE ONE WHO FLIPS THE SWITCH TO FRY THESE BASTARDS. IN FACT, I WOULD PAY A GREAT DEAL OF MONEY FOR THE PRIVILEGE.

SINCERELY
ARTHUR GABLES
PORTLAND, ORE.

DEAD END

Institutionalized death has a way of creeping under our skin and penetrating our senses like a drug. The death penalty anesthetizes. It lives with us, changes us, saddens us, weakens us. Its wounds are hard to heal. Some may never go away, even if the death penalty is abolished forever.

CHAPTER 1
THE ROAD

"Mom, they can't find Amy Sue."
—Patti Linebaugh, relating her daughter's comments on the day Patti's granddaughter was abducted and tortured to death.

"I feel morally and intellectually obligated simply to concede that the death penalty experiment has failed."
— U.S. Supreme Court Justice Harry Blackmun, February, 1994.

San Quentin, CA — The rain fell hard on the families of the condemned, a somber addition to worn and tired faces.

That's how it started — an innocent sentence in a newspaper story. Not the kind of thing to make much fuss over; not the kind of sentence that could change a life. But it did. It changed mine.

A few months earlier, before I assembled those words on my flickering video display terminal, I was a wide-eyed journalism school graduate from the University of Missouri who had returned home to Southern California to pursue my career. While at Missouri, I covered the state's prison system and Death Row for my school paper, as well as for United Press International. My first love was politics, and I had a feeling that because of the prevailing electoral wind toward being "tough" on crime, my collegiate encounters with capital punishment would not be my last.

I was right. Shortly after taking a job with a mid-sized daily newspaper in Ventura County, a relatively quiet enclave adjacent to Los Angeles, the state announced that it was preparing to execute its first inmate in 23 years. We were just a small newspaper, but I felt we had to give the story some kind of special treatment because of the significance of the impending event. And I knew that I was the one who should do it.

That probably sounds somewhat cocky, but the truth is I truly was uniquely qualified. In Missouri, I covered that state's first execution in more than two decades. This was my story, my issue. For some reason, I felt stronger about this story than I did about any other I'd written before.

My editors ultimately succumbed to my annoying enthusiasm and agreed to let me do a story, provided I worked in some local angles. But when they balked at sending me to San Quentin, where the gas chamber is located, I decided that I would travel the 300 miles at my own expense.

I didn't have any interviews lined up, nor was I exactly sure what I was going to do once I got there. I just knew that if I was going to write about capital punishment in California, I needed to go where capital punishment happened.

When I saw the families in the visiting area getting soaked while hoping for a chance to see their condemned relatives, I knew I had made the right decision. It became the perfect backdrop from which to tell my story.

My focus for the article was the controversy over streamlining the appeals process, and how public frustration with a seemingly snail-paced punishment had prompted some politicians to shorten the road to Death Row. It was the same kind of frustration that we're seeing today as the public and the political establishment once again turn their attention toward crime and public safety issues.

In my story, I pointed out that limiting the appeals process could lead innocent men to their deaths. Former California Governor Edmund G. "Pat" Brown told me, "the more I saw (death penalty) cases, the more I was against capital punishment." Perhaps my best quote, however, came from Ursula, a stout German gardener whom I saw pulling weeds less than 100 yards from the San Quentin Prison gates. Looking at her made you smile — listening to her made you think.

"People here aren't as educated as we are in Europe; they don't think things through or rationalize what justice is," she said. "All they say is, 'Just kill 'em! C'mon, just kill 'em all!' "

A couple of months after I wrote that story, in the spring of 1990, I was sitting in my newspaper office with U.S. Senator Dianne Feinstein of California, who was then running for the Democratic gubernatorial nomination. (She eventually lost to California Gov. Pete Wilson.) The execution of Robert Alton Harris was only a few weeks away, and his impending gassing had been the talk of the campaign. All of the candidates were trying furiously to position themselves as the toughest proponents of capital punishment. A man's life, no matter how worthless some thought it was, had been unceremoniously reduced to campaign fodder.

"We have to carry out the people's will that they voted for 11 years ago on the death penalty," Feinstein told me, as her aide, Dee Dee Myers (later President Clinton's Press Secretary), took copious notes. "As unpleasant as it is, the state has had enough of serial murder, of mayhem, of rape, of brutality.

"While serving on the parole board, I had a woman come before me in a case of robbery in the first degree. And I noticed that she had an unloaded gun during the robbery. And I asked her the question, 'Why was the gun unloaded?' And she said to me, 'So I wouldn't panic, kill somebody, and get the death penalty.'

"That was my first direct testimony that the death penalty is, in fact, a deterrent to crime. I very much believe it is a deterrent to crime, and that the people's will should be carried out."

Well, Feinstein came and went, and so did Harris' appointment with the gas chamber. And as quickly as it had become the hottest issue of the gubernatorial campaign, capital punishment was pushed off the front page. The denizens of Death Row were forgotten right along with it.

As soon as the death penalty was no longer convenient, it was ignored. The real issues — cost, deterrence, fairness — were never addressed by the politicians and anointed opinion leaders. As the summer wore on, I realized that an honest, open dialogue on the death penalty was simply not going to happen.

Even my colleagues in the media weren't going to talk to those affected by capital punishment or dig into the issues surrounding the ultimate, most irreversible of government actions. The answer was painfully clear: if I wanted to read an in-depth report on capital punishment, I would have to write it myself.

If it were only that simple! To do it right, I would need time — weeks, maybe evens months. I would need to travel; the phone was too impersonal. Eventually, what began as an interest turned into a story, and the story soon developed into an obsession.

I got up the courage to ask my editors for a leave of absence to compile my research, and I must admit I wasn't at all surprised when they declined. They were definitely surprised, however, when I told them I was resigning. The story — the obsession — had now become more important than my salary and my professional future.

I spent the next month making a flurry of phone calls, trying to set up as many interviews as possible before embarking on a cross-country road trip. Slowly, my itinerary started to come together — Washington D.C., Virginia, Illinois, Missouri. But mostly I was counting on luck and divine intervention to guide my way. I was going to have to wing it. It was a scary proposition, to be sure — no job, no financial security, no guarantees.

Yet as I said good-bye to my co-workers on a warm Southern California day in late October 1990, there were no regrets, either. I was frightened of the future, though by that time, with so much invested in my journey both personally and professionally, the only thing I feared more than moving forward was turning back.

The first question one editor asked when I told her of my plans was one I expected: Why the death penalty?

Although I was opposed to the death penalty, I felt no sympathy for the people on Death Row. Most of them, like Theodore Frank, deserved to rot out their lives in jail for what they did, and society deserved to be protected from them.

No one felt sympathy for Theodore Frank, the most notorious killer ever to come out of Ventura County and the catalyst that led to the ouster of liberal California Supreme Court Justice Rose Bird in 1986, a vehement death penalty opponent.

Frank, a 43-year-old former mental patient, was a known child molester. He had been released from a program for mentally disordered sex offenders less than two months before he abducted 2-year-old Amy Sue Seitz from her baby-sitter's front yard on March 14, 1978.

That morning, Frank drove his wife to work and then went to Amy's Camarillo neighborhood, which was nearby. He picked up Amy, drove to a secluded area, and proceeded to molest her in a variety of ways: he pulled her nipples with a pliers-like instrument; he hit her on the head, scratched her chest with a knife and tore the opening of her vagina; he inserted a foreign object into her anus, and then strangled her.

The next day, Amy's mutilated body was found on the lawn of a Topanga Canyon home in nearby Los Angeles County.

"Because of the discoloration and mutilation, we couldn't make a positive identification," Patti Linebaugh, Amy's grandmother, told me shortly before I embarked on my trip. "We went back to my house and lifted prints there, and those prints matched. To this day, I still get the fingerprint granules off of our coffee table.

"When my daughter called and said, 'Mom, they can't find Amy Sue,' I thought things would be fine. The last thing on my mind was that someone like Theodore Frank would have abducted Amy.

"You can't understand unless you go through it," Patti said. "The emotion, the non-belief, the outrage, the grief. It has a long-term effect on you. I still have in the house a deodorant bottle that Amy used to love to play with because of the shape. You don't throw those things away."

Patti co-chaired the committee to oust Rose Bird and several other justices who had joined with Bird to block numerous death penalty cases, 57 in all. Although Patti said she feels for the families of the condemned and admitted they, too, are victims in this process, she also feels that the true definition of the word "justice" would be the death of Theodore Frank.

"As far as I'm concerned, he relinquished all right to life when he did what he did to that child," Patti said. "When he is killed, I will feel that justice will have finally prevailed. You will still live with the loss of Amy, but he will have paid the penalty for his crime.

"I just want this over," Patti said. "I'm not obsessed with waiting for Theodore Frank to die. If the court decided to reverse the death penalty, fine. Let's just get it over."

Frank was convicted in 1980, but his death sentence was overturned by Bird's court because of illegally seized evidence. Frank received a new death sentence in 1987; he was still on Death Row when I headed onto the open highway for Washington, D.C.

In my mind, trepidation hung in the cool fall air as I pulled out of my driveway, my Acura hatchback packed with research papers, an Apple computer, two suitcases, and a hearty supply of canned tuna and bottled water. These perhaps weren't the supplies of a seasoned explorer, but I felt they were sufficient for the task before me: a cross-country journey into America's death-penalty subculture. The nation's capital was going to be my first stop, not for symbolic reasons, but for practical ones.

Washington was playing host to the National Coalition to Abolish the Death Penalty's annual conference, and many of the people whom I wanted to interview would all be in the same hotel on the same weekend. Some, like Virginia para-legal Marie Deans, I already had spoken to by phone from California. Marie, who opposes the death penalty despite her mother-in-law's brutal murder, was arranging an interview for me with one of her clients on Virginia's Death Row.

Others, like Tennessee preacher Joe Ingle, I wasn't able to contact until I was already on the road. When I finally reached him at the Southern Coalition on Jails and Prisons, of which he was director, he said he wanted to meet with me at the conference before deciding to go any further with an interview. I then asked him if it was possible for me to meet with some of the inmates on Tennessee's Death Row.

"That depends on whether I let you on (Death Row) or not," Joe said. "Why don't we just talk first and let me get to know you better. I don't let just anybody on Death Row."

Joe's reluctance to let me into his world was the same kind of resistance I felt from other self-proclaimed death penalty abolitionists. Clive Smith, a death penalty lawyer whom I was able to arrange an interview with in Atlanta, gave me the third degree during a 30-minute phone conversation before he agreed to the interview.

Once they understood that I was no great fan of the death penalty, my problems subsided. You almost had to be completely on their side for them to help you, it seemed, or else you would not be admitted into their world. On the outside, after all, the death penalty is viewed much differently. The people who oppose it have created a culture, a way of life all their own, and have nothing to gain by someone from the outside coming in to tear it down.

You don't need to be a history scholar to know that the moral and ethical dilemmas of capital punishment date back to the beginning of time.

The arguments for the death penalty were as simple in biblical times as they are now: an eye for an eye. If you kill, you should be killed. That's actually the way it's been throughout most of western civilization. First, people were killed in public. Who could forget the Christians and the lions, or the prairie justice of the Wild West? Eventually, as society began to see itself as more civilized, executions were moved indoors and away from public view. Communal stonings gave way to restrained execution rituals. The last meal and opportunity to say a few parting words were added to give the ordeal dignity.

The method of execution also changed. Stoning led to hanging and firing squads, which then led to the electric chair, the gas chamber and now, lethal injection. Although the electric chair is still the most popular way to execute people, many states are currently replacing their chairs with lethal injection, which is viewed as the most humane mode of execution. Some gas chamber states are opting to give inmates a choice between gas or injection. Hanging and firing squads are still used in Washington and Utah.

The 1930s and '40s were banner decades for executions in the United States. In 1935, there were 195 executions. From 1930 through 1949, there were 2,951 total executions, which averages out to 148 per year.

During the time the United States was executing people in record numbers, the rest of the western world was abolishing its death penalty laws. The practice was viewed by countries throughout Europe as barbaric and ineffective in reducing violent crime. Today, South Africa is the only other western democracy that still has a death penalty.

A total of 3,859 people were executed from 1930 to 1967, when on April 12th of that year, 37-year-old Aaron C. Mitchell was gassed in California for killing a police officer. As it turned out, it would be the last execution in the United States for a decade.

After Aaron Mitchell's execution, growing public opposition to the death penalty prompted the United States Supreme Court to declare capital punishment "cruel and unusual punishment," and therefore unconstitutional, in the landmark Furman vs. Georgia decision in 1972. But instead of backing off, states, mostly those in the South, immediately began re-writing their statutes so that they wouldn't have to turn their execution chambers into museums.

In 1976, the Supreme Court upheld the revised capital punishment laws, and the race was on to see which state would be the first to usher in a new era in American executions. Utah got the nod on January 17, 1977, when Gary Gilmore was executed by firing squad. It was another two years before the next execution, that of Florida's John Spenkelink on May 25, 1979. That same year, Nevada executed Jesse Bishop.

The drought, it seemed, was over. There was one execution in 1981, two in 1982 and five in 1983. But as more and more cases ran their course of appeals, the floodgates broke open with 21 executions in 1984; currently, around 30 to 40 people are executed annually. Since the death penalty was reinstated in 1976, more than 235 people have been executed by hanging, firing squad, electrocution, gas, and lethal injection.

As I stated before, my opposition to the death penalty doesn't come from any kind of love or compassion for criminals. I don't want these guys running around the streets killing innocent people, including this innocent person. There are numerous issues involved, not the least of which are moral and philosophical. Primarily, however, my opposition to the death penalty comes from the facts.

Many people support capital punishment because they believe it is a deterrent to violent crime, although there is no concrete evidence to support that claim. According to the FBI, states that have abolished the death penalty average 4.9 murders per 100,000 population, while the 38 states with death penalty statutes average 7.9 murders.

In California, there were no executions and 897 homicides in 1966. One year later, after 37-year-old Aaron C. Mitchell was executed for killing a police officer, the murder rate climbed to 1,051.

Who is on Death Row? About 20,000 people commit murder each year in the United States, with about 2,800 people on Death Row — the largest number in any nation in history. A few are serial killers, like Richard Ramirez in California and John Wayne Gacey, recently executed in Illinois, but most of them have killed only once, and some of them never even pulled the trigger.

Almost every one of those 2,800 are poor and are on Death Row because they couldn't afford competent legal counsel. If you're rich, you don't go to Death Row. It's as simple as that. If you're poor, your attorney is liable to be either young and inexperienced, or old and incompetent.

According to the National Law Journal, "Indigent defendants on trial for their lives are being frequently represented by ill-trained, unprepared, court-appointed lawyers." In six Southern states — Alabama, Georgia, Florida, Louisiana, Mississippi, and Texas — the Journal says death penalty trial lawyers have been disbarred, suspended or disciplined at 3 to 46 times the overall rate for those states.

Part of the problem is that in order to find competent lawyers, you have to pay them. But the reality is that death penalty cases pay little to nothing. In 1992, an American Bar Association study found that lawyers who take on death cases can expect to lose anywhere from $250,000 to one million per case.

One death case in Georgia was tried (and lost) by a third-year law student, and in four other trials that led to Death Row, the defense attorneys referred to their clients in open court as "niggers".

Said the late U.S. Supreme Court Justice Thurgood Marshall: "The task of eliminating arbitrariness in the infliction of capital punishment is proving to be one which our criminal justice system — and perhaps any criminal justice system — is unable to perform." In a stunning statement issued by U.S. Supreme Court Justice Harry A. Blackmun in February, 1994, the jurist who voted to restore capital punishment in 1976 declared that "the death penalty, as currently administered, is unconstitutional. Rather than continue to coddle the court's delusion that the desired level of fairness has been achieved and the need for regulation eviscerated, I feel morally and intellectually obligated simply to concede that the death penalty experiment has failed.

"The problem," Blackmun said, "is that the inevitability of factual, legal and moral error gives us a system that we know must wrongly kill some defendants, a system that fails to deliver the fair, consistent and reliable sentences of death required by the Constitution."

A 1987 Stanford Law Review study revealed that at least 23 people executed this century in the United States were killed in error, either because they were innocent or tried unjustly. Another 22 came within 72 hours of execution.

Since the '70s, at least 37 people have been released after many years on Death Row because they were discovered to be innocent. One of the most famous cases is that of Randall Dale Adams, a Texas inmate freed in 1989 following 12 years on Death Row, after the documentary A *Thin Blue Line* proved that Adams was not a killer. Clarence Brandley, a black Texas inmate, was released in 1990 after a decade on Death Row when two white prosecution witnesses admitted that a white man had committed the crime.

Race, especially in the South, plays a major role in regard to who gets executed. Although half of all murder victims are black, 85 percent of those executed since 1977, as well as those awaiting execution, were charged with killing whites. Only twice in the long history of U.S. executions has a white person been executed for killing a black.

Perhaps the statistic that's most shocking is that it costs more to kill somebody than to keep them in prison for life. Sure, our tax dollars feed and clothe inmates, but they also pay for prosecutors, public defenders, judges, and everything else that's involved in a capital case. Capital murder trials, because of the high stakes involved, simply take longer to prepare and conduct than other murder trials. And limiting the federal appeals process, a popular sentiment among judges and prosecutors, won't change anything. Even before the appeals process begins, we've already spent at least twice as much to try a death penalty case than it would cost to house an inmate for life.

Tax payers in Texas, for example, pay an average of $2.3 million per death penalty case, which is about three times the cost of imprisoning someone in a single cell at the highest security penitentiary for 40 years. In Florida, each execution costs the state $3.2 million. California could save $90 million a year by eliminating the death penalty; Kansas recently dropped its death penalty because of the cost. The more money put into death cases, the less there is for victims' families and police protection.

"If we didn't have to pay $500,000 a pop for Sacramento's murders, I would have an investigator and the sheriff would have a couple of extra deputies, and we could do some lasting good for Sierra County law enforcement," said Sierra County, California district attorney James Reichle about a 1988 cut in police services due to death penalty prosecutions. "The sewage system at the court house is failing, a bridge collapsed, there's no county library, no county park, and we have volunteer fire and volunteer search and rescue."

But what do you do with these murderers if not kill them?

Most people, when presented with the alternative of life in prison without the possibility of parole, choose imprisonment over execution. A 1991 survey in Massachusetts showed that 71 percent supported capital punishment. But when respondents were informed that the alternative was life without parole, support for the death penalty dipped to 44 percent. Similar results were found in polls conducted by the U.S. Justice Department and in a California survey, where life without parole is the only other sentencing option in capital cases.

The bottom line in this ongoing debate is that people simply want to feel safe — we certainly deserve to be safe from those who commit murder. We just may not have to kill them to give us peace of mind.

But enough statistics. I didn't go on this trip to compile more data or write a term paper. I was looking for the emotions behind the numbers. I wanted to see if my feelings were right — and if not, why they were wrong.

THE ROAD

On my drive to Washington, which happened to be just before the November elections, the major issues being debated on talk radio shows were the economy, abortion, and the death penalty. I had plenty of time to think about what I might find as I wove my way across the Rockies and through America's heartland. There's nothing like an open road to free your soul, stretch your imagination and remind you that the world is wider than the confines of your daily routine. We should be reminded more often.

My trip east was pretty uneventful, save for my conversation with Joe Ingle and a stop in Columbia, Missouri, for an oil change and visit with my fiancee, Christine. It wasn't until I saw her that I realized my trip wasn't just about me, but her, too.

We were planning on getting married in only seven months, and here I was quitting my job to travel at my own expense, with nothing lined up for when it was all over. This is not a terribly effective way to endear yourself to your future in-laws. I was afraid they might call off the wedding by reason of insanity.

Everyone said they understood, that this was something I needed to do and that now was the best time to do it. But how could they understand it if I didn't understand it myself? More than a few times I thought about ending the trip right there in Missouri and foregoing my self-imposed exile. I had family, I had friends, and I had a soon-to-be wife who loved me so much that she would let me travel around the United States by myself and spend all of the money I should have been saving to begin our life together.

But I knew I had to go, and so did she. I promised to call when I could, and send the occasional postcard. It took every ounce of courage I had to drive away from that face, that image of comfort and security. It seems strange to think about it now, but it was as if she were pushing me to leave, aware that I couldn't do it on my own. And because of that, I knew that while I was going to be by myself for quite some time, I was never going to be alone.

I drove contentedly for the next few hours, as day turned to night and Missouri gave way to Illinois. I wanted to get to Indianapolis before stopping for the night, which meant about five more hours of driving in what had to have been the darkest night on record in the Midwest.

I'm pretty good about staying awake on the road, and I rarely have to pull over for a nap. I'm also pretty stubborn, and tend to drive longer than I should. This was one of those nights. I really was exhausted. It had been an emotional day, and my mind was working overtime. My headlights did little to direct my path, illuminating the lines in the road only seconds before I passed them.

Suddenly, something happened that jolted me awake and kept me that way until Indianapolis. A bright, golden light appeared behind me, and it was gaining — fast. It wasn't a headlight from another car or a police vehicle. As it got closer, I could see that it was a cross, barreling up at 75 mph — that was it, just a cross, traveling by itself. Perhaps my drowsy brain was playing tricks on me, but I could have sworn that the cross was coming right for me, trying desperately to catch up. Maybe it was an omen, trying to warn me about some unforeseen danger. Maybe it wanted to pass and lead me to my destination safely. Maybe it was telling me to rethink my political views!

I was becoming quite alarmed by the time it closed in on my rear bumper. Finally, in the dark Illinois night, I could see that the cross was attached to the grill of an 18-wheeler. Feeling somewhat foolish and vastly relieved, I let it pass me and followed it all the way to Indianapolis. I never did feel tired after that.

I drove a total of four days, including my trip from California to Missouri, and arrived in Washington around 4 p.m. on a Friday afternoon. After fighting through rush hour traffic and a barely working knowledge of the D.C. area, I found a parking space alongside the Howard Inn, down the street from Howard University and 10 minutes from Capitol Hill.

THE ROAD

I locked my car and tugged my trench coat collar over my chilled ears. As I turned toward the hotel, a light rain, reminiscent of the one that fell on the families of the condemned in San Quentin, moistened my face.

CHAPTER 2

FAMILY REUNION

"I didn't marry a man on Death Row. I married Bobby."
— November West, wife of Texas Death Row inmate Bobby West.

"I oppose the death penalty not for the inmates' sake, but for our sake. We know who the inmates are — the question is who we are."

— Henry Schwarzschild, head of the ACLU's Capital Punishment Project.

My first stop was the main ballroom to see if anything was going on, and anything wasn't. People were still registering and milling about, reminiscing and reintroducing themselves to old friends. I felt like I was crashing a family reunion, and in many ways I was.

After about a half-hour of mingling, I learned that a meeting of people who had marched from Death Row in Starke, Florida, to Atlanta in opposition to the death penalty was going on upstairs. I decided to drop in and meet some of the marchers.

The small conference room was filled with about 40 people sitting in a half-circle, eyes glued to a slide show of the march. People shouted over the taped narration whenever they saw themselves on the screen, marching in solidarity through tiny towns and large urban centers. Some cried, while others wondered when they could do it again.

The presentation ended with a slide of the Rev. Joseph Lowery, head of the Southern Christian Leadership Conference, delivering a speech at a rally for the marchers in Atlanta:

"More than one-half of the persons on Death Row are in the South," the reverend boomed. "Georgia is among the bottom five in education, and among the top four in execution. The time has come for us to renounce violence as a means of resolving violence."

After the slide show, everyone went around the room and told the group what they had learned from the pilgrimage march, and what they were doing now. There was Bob Doemer, a former Death Row inmate from Ohio; Sam Sheppard, the son of a murder victim; and Dan Horowitz, who described himself as a concerned citizen from Florida.

Dan said that before the infamous Ted Bundy's execution, he was very much pro death penalty and openly advocated Bundy's death. But all that changed when the crowds massed to celebrate Bundy's electrocution.

"I remember turning on the local news and seeing the people outside the prison," he said. "They were screaming, cheering, waving frying pans and drinking beer. McDonald's was giving away free french fries.

"At that moment, Ted Bundy was free, and I was trapped. This kind of vengeance, this cycle of violence is what I was going to have to live with."

The most interesting person at the meeting was a woman named November West. Short and plump, she had Tiny Tim's hair and a grandmother's smile. She described herself as a "political poet" from Greenwich Village, and declared that she was married to a man on Death Row in Texas.

She was a little eccentric, with her Salvation Army wardrobe and costume jewelry, yet I sensed a sincere warmth and down-to-earth quality about this unemployed schoolteacher who writes poems about Death Row. She agreed to meet with me later in the evening and talk about her husband.

The conference opened with little fanfare, saving the best for Saturday when Joe Ingle and Marie Deans were to receive Abolitionist of the Year awards. After about an hour-long discussion on "Race, Politics and the Death Penalty", the tired went to bed and the hearty went to the bar.

I was exhausted, but I went to the bar anyway. I sat at a table with a group of abolitionists, including Sister Helen Prejean, the first nun I've ever seen in a bar and who drank Budweiser like it was holy water.

November walked in a few minutes later, gave me a smile and invited me to talk. Above the din of the noisy hotel bar, November, in her thickest Irish-New York accent, gave me an earful.

"To me, murder is always an irrational act," she said. "Nobody in their right mind ever decides to kill somebody. It's an insane act. Of course I don't believe that somebody like Ted Bundy should be allowed to run out and kill somebody else's daughter, but I do think we need to study people like Ted Bundy, and keep them from harming other people.

"We're not prepared to look at the Gandhi and Hitler inside ourselves, and that's a fact. Think about your life, and think about the times you wanted to do something to somebody, hit or slap somebody. At that time, something in our chemical make-up made us do that, and later we regretted it, right? It's not rational to do stuff like that.

"All murders are committed either from anger, or drugs, alcohol, or feeling there's no way out. They're all irrational situations. We're all capable of both, Gandhi and Hitler, all the time."

November continued to rant about the American legal system, and I listened patiently, even though that's not what I wanted to talk about. What I wanted to talk about was her husband, Bobby West, and when I finally got the chance to broach the subject, November's ranting turned to reflection.

"His best friend was killed," November said, explaining how Bobby got to Death Row. "He went out to these people, the ones responsible for his friend's death, put one of them in the hospital and he died. That's not a capital crime, it's a revenge murder. Bobby is on Death Row largely because he had a stupid lawyer who's now prepared to stand up in court and say he didn't defend Bobby properly.

"Bobby killed somebody. But it's not a capital crime. Even the guards down there don't understand it. I asked Bobby if he felt better after the killing, and he said 'absolutely not.' He was just in pain."

November threw my next question back into my face. I asked her why she married a man on Death Row.

"I didn't marry a man on Death Row," November said, raising her eyebrows. "I married Bobby."

I apologized and hoped I didn't offend her too badly. But November shrugged it off, gave me one of those grandmother smiles and bought the next round of drinks.

November said she met Bobby through an article in the Catholic Worker magazine soliciting prisoner pen pals. She sent him a Christmas card, and Bobby promptly wrote back. After three months of exchanging letters, November decided to go to Texas and meet this man in person.

"He looked exactly the same as the descriptions in his letters," she said. "There was about a foot of glass between us. We talked, and then he said we should go to California, because then we could have conjugal visits. But I said to do that you'd have to be married. 'Are you telling me you want to get married?' I asked. He dropped it like that."

They continued to write, and eventually November went to Texas to see him again. This time, marriage was the main topic of conversation.

"I said, 'Bobby, you're forgetting something. You never asked me.' He said, 'You're right. Will you marry me?' I said yes.

"Well, I immediately went to the courthouse and asked them how to go about it, and I filled out all the necessary forms," November said of the happiest day of her life. "I met a woman who agreed to stand in for Bobby at the ceremony. I really didn't think I was going to go through with it, but I did.

"The strangest part was that I had to do it before a judge, and when he asked if I would have this man to have and to hold, I realized that I had never touched Bobby's hand. I still haven't. Anyway, afterward I went back to the prison and held up the marriage certificate to the glass for Bobby to see. We were married."

I asked November whether she thought she would ever touch her husband's hand.

"I'll touch him when he gets out," she said as her lips turned up in a smile. "When he gets out."

I spent the night at a friend's house in Maryland. After five hours of sleep on a wooden floor, I was back at the hotel by 8 a.m. for a full day of work.

The morning calendar consisted of a series of workshops on how to be a more effective abolitionist. To be honest, it wasn't very exciting. Much of the discussion focused on technical aspects of basic lobbying techniques, which offered me no great revelations into the minds of the conference attendees. I felt guilty for not paying full attention to what was going on, and I was a little sleepy from the night before. As my eyes wandered around the room, however, I noticed I wasn't the only one having trouble maintaining interest.

It took me a second to get a clear view, but as the man turned and walked out of the room, I knew instantly from the long face and longer forehead that it was Henry Schwarzschild.

I first met Henry in the waning weeks before Gerald Smith's scheduled execution in Missouri. A lawyer with the ACLU, Henry is a nationally recognized leader of the abolitionist move-ment, whose booming, mile-a-minute patter has silenced scores of death penalty advocates in national debates. The most interesting thing about Henry is that, unlike most other abolitionists, he refuses to have any affection or sympathy for people on Death Row. He simply feels that governments should not be in the business of killing their own citizens.

I figured if Henry Schwarzschild could walk out of the workshop, so could I. Henry was the founder and first director of the National Coalition to Abolish the Death Penalty. I guess he was entitled. After a few minutes of searching, I found him in the hotel lounge, smoking a cigarette and staring into space. Now director of the ACLU's Capital Punishment Project, he was gracious enough to let me join him, and even more willing to talk about capital punishment.

I made sure my tape recorder had fresh batteries, because if anybody could wear out a pair of Duracells, Henry Schwarzschild was the person to do it. I started by asking him whether he felt somewhat of an outsider at the conference because he doesn't share the same compassion for Death Row inmates as do many of his colleagues.

"I think it is politically wiser and morally safer not to sentimentalize the people on Death Row," Henry said. "It's better if I think they are as contemptible as the Florida attorney general does, and I still don't want them executed. I oppose the death penalty not for the inmates' sake, but for our sake. We know who the inmates are — the question is who we are. We ought to be too civilized to do this sort of thing.

"I don't want to have to worry about whether Death Row inmates are nice guys or not," he said. "This way I can have a clean shot at opposing the death penalty."

I tried to get in another question, but it was useless. He was on a roll.

"No one opposes the death penalty because we think the people who commit murders are nice people," Henry said. "Of course they're not, of course the things they did were bad. I don't think they're heroes, or saints, I don't think they're wonderful. I think that, by and large, they are miserably pathological people who have done terrible things and who society ought to protect itself against. In fact, I demand it. I'd just as soon kill 'em as everybody else.

"But I don't think that a racially neutral death penalty is any better that a racially discriminatory one. I don't think an error-free death penalty is any better than one that's bound to make mistakes. The question is whether you think political institutions should be in the business of killing folks, and the answer to that is very clearly no. Because when they do, the only question that remains is not whether killing is intolerable, but who is doing the killing.

"Execution is worse than homicide. With homicide, we know that people are not always rational and are very often destructive. But governments ought not be irrational, ought not be destructive, and therefore ought not be killing people — especially when it doesn't do any good.

"Governments ought not have the power to decide who lives or who dies," Henry said, taking a breath to drag on his cigarette. "The state is a deeply inappropriate institution to decide that."

Henry, in his mid-60's, came to the United States from Germany in 1939, and after earning a degree in political theory from Columbia University, worked in counter-intelligence for the U.S. Army during World War II. He has held numerous positions throughout his career, not the least of which were stints with the U.S. State Department, and his work on desegration with civil rights leaders such as Dr. Martin Luther King Jr.

Through it all, he has seen many sides of the death penalty debate. And like any good debater, he does his best to understand the positions of his opponents.

"This is an extremely macho society," Henry said. "We think that every problem that confronts this country will yield if you're just tough enough to deal with it, and I think the reason for this is the Vietnam War. We were defeated in that war by a bunch of fucking mountain tribes in a country that no one could find on a map. Since then, we've been trying to show everybody that, dammit, we are tough.

"The death penalty is just another gesture of machismo. The fear makes them think that toughness is the universal solvent of all problems. People are fearful for their lives and families, and they are very angry at a criminal justice system that they think doesn't work very well.

"Because of this fear," he said, "the death penalty is going to be with us for a very long time. I think the death penalty will survive my lifetime very nicely. That's too bad. But I'm not in charge, and all I can do is say my piece."

As Henry finished his sentence, a tall, bearded man walked up to our table. I didn't know the face, but I knew the name. Everybody in the abolitionist movement knows the name.

"Gary, do you know Hugo Bedau?" Henry said. I smiled sheepishly and introduced myself, and made some stupid comment about how much I admired his work. He probably thought I was going to ask for an autograph.

Hugo, most would agree, is the father of the abolitionist movement. The beard makes him look like a guru, but he is too much the academic for that kind of role. Now chair of the philosophy department at Tufts University, Hugo, in the early '60s, wrote the first comprehensive overview on capital punishment, titled *The Death Penalty in America*. It is a scholarly treatise that has been updated three times, and remains the leading resource for historians and researchers. He since has written several other books on the legal and moral aspects of capital punishment.

I had planned on tracking him down at the conference, so it was a pleasant surprise when he inadvertently tracked me down instead. But it was even more surprising — shocking, actually — when he invited me to lunch with him and his wife.

Henry excused himself, saying he had a meeting to attend. So the patriarch of the abolitionist movement and I walked over to the crowded hotel restaurant, found his wife waiting at a table, and sat down for some food and conversation.

My first question was easy: Why did he decide to write the definitive research book on capital punishment?

"In 1958, there wasn't anybody except a very small number who were experts on any aspect of the death penalty," Hugo said. "I taught myself everything I needed to know as rapidly as I could.

"The book was an attempt to provide a comprehensive document on all aspects of the death penalty in the United States. It was a semi-encyclopedia. Much of it was reprinted from journals and other publications, and the other 10 or 15 percent I wrote myself.

"The death penalty for me has really required a major shift in my perception on how to think about a problem. I was aware of the civil rights movements in the early '50s; I was an angry opponent of the Eisenhower era, but I really didn't understand anything about complex social and legal issues until I got involved in this issue.

"I wasn't really against the death penalty in the beginning, but I didn't know why I would be in favor of it, either. After I started reading about it, I knew I was against it. It was all or nothing, and it became nothing real fast."

Hugo said the main issue back in the '50s was trying to get the individual state legislatures to abolish the death penalty. The abolitionists had some success, though some states, such as Delaware, brought it back a few years later.

In the '60s, the focus changed. The ACLU and NAACP, both fixtures in the fight for civil rights, came out and said the death penalty was a violation of "fundamental civil rights and civil liberties." This marked the first time that abolitionists would go after the death penalty on purely constitutional grounds, now a common occurrence in death penalty appeals known as the Writ of Habeas Corpus — an attempt to stop an execution because of a constitutional violation. The U.S. Supreme Court has since acted to limit the number of Habeas appeals that can be filed, arguing that they serve only to delay the inevitable.

Hugo explained that everything crystallized in the landmark 1972 Furman decision. And then, almost immediately, all the abolitionists had worked for began falling apart.

"It seemed that the death penalty got reinstated overnight," Hugo said. "In 1964, the same year my book came out, the death penalty was defeated at the polls in Oregon. That was a high water mark in public attitude and opinion in opposing the death penalty.

"But between Furman and Gregg, there was a lot of agitation around the country to bring back the death penalty. Support for the death penalty has always been code for two things: one is 'this is a way to put blacks and other minorities in their place and control them,' and the other is 'give the authority and power to us in government, and we'll protect you.' Politicians now see that supporting the death penalty is a way of saying, 'I care about you. And whoever doesn't support it, doesn't care about you.'

"The support for the death penalty is a mile wide and an inch deep," Hugo said, his eyes now searching the restaurant for our food. "The public does not massively support killing prisoners under the law. They say they do when you ask them, but then they go right on and want another beer so they can go back to their crossword puzzle. It's not something with which people have intense beliefs."

Our meals finally arrived, and our stomachs immediately told us it was time to stop talking. We finished our lunch without any more conversation about the death penalty, and I was a little relieved. This stuff gets to you after a while, and sometimes you need a break.

It's a good thing, too. Next on my agenda was a workshop headed by Marie Deans, and I knew that would plunge me right back into the emotional thick of things.

Marie Deans is one of those characters you'd expect to find in a short story. She is a hard-talking, no-nonsense product of the American South, so much a caricature of the region that she is unique. Beneath the hard exterior of a Louisiana woman doing battle against the forces of ignorance in Virginia, there are the tears of a bereaved relative, and the gentle power of compassion and love.

While pregnant with her now teen-age son, Robert, Marie's mother-in-law, Penny, was murdered. A man followed her home one day, and after a brief struggle, shot her twice. The man eventually was found and charged with the murder, and is serving a life sentence in Maine where there is no death penalty. Yet the murder changed Marie's life forever, and she decided two things: she wanted to learn more about the people who commit these horrible crimes, and she didn't want any more people to die, including those on Death Row.

Marie founded a group called Murder Victims' families for Reconciliation, became a para-legal and now is director of the Virginia Coalition on Jails and Prisons. She is solely responsible for convincing many a hardcore criminal to pick up his appeals and not give up on life.

I talked to Marie a few times on the phone before I left California. She was nice enough to set up an interview with me and one of her favorite and most famous clients, Joe Giarratano. He was on Death Row for a crime he and thousands throughout the world, including M*A*S*H actor Mike Farrell and conservative newspaper columnist James Kilpatrick, said he didn't commit.

But for now, it was time to listen to Marie do what she does best: teach people how to care about the men and women on Death Row.

The small workshop room was packed, the awestruck audience hanging on her every syllable. It was akin to a group of college basketball players getting some playing tips from Michael Jordan, or a group of actors listening to Sir Lawrence Olivier tell them how to perform Hamlet. Unknown to the rest of the world, here Marie Deans was a superstar.

Marie said that the most important thing to remember in dealing with inmates on Death Row is that whether you like them or not, you have to love them.

"This is about their life, and whether it's going to be saved. You have to balance that with your own anger and your own determination, and if you're not angry, then you've got to find somebody who is.

"Here's somebody that wants to jump off the roof, and you don't want him to jump off the roof, and he's fighting with you... that ought to make you angry. When I go in there, I'm mad, I'm angry and I'm determined. He's a human being, he's my brother, and I don't want his life snuffed out by anybody."

Marie said she sometimes shows her determination by not being afraid to use foul language — something inmates wouldn't expect from a slender, frail looking Southern lady.

"I have a real filthy mouth; bad language doesn't bother me at all," she said. "When someone tells me they're tired, I've suffered enough, I have no problem saying, 'Who the fuck do you think you are? What are you telling me you're tired? You fucked up, and you've got to do something about it. And suicide is not the proper solution.'

"You've got to care about him, and never ever give up. I would follow them into the death chamber holding onto their toes, because somewhere along the line he may change his mind. You do not leave them down there, you do not stop, you just keep going."

After the workshop, I went up to Marie and thanked her for arranging the interview for me with Joe. I then asked her whether, because of her overbearing attitude toward the inmates, Joe or any other inmate has ever refused to see her.

"Well, they're scared to do that," she said. "One inmate tried to do that, and I called him a chicken shit. I did it on the Row, so all of his friends could hear me.

"This is my style," she said, half-apologizing for her colorful language. "Some people can do this by being nice, but I can't. I'm angry. I'm angry about this whole thing."

Sam Sheppard was angry too. So angry, in fact, that he spent most of his adult life as far away from society as possible. When he was seven-years-old, his mother was beaten to death while he was in the house. His father was tried and convicted of the crime, and spent time on Death Row before being acquitted in a subsequent trial.

The experience has given Sam a unique perspective, that of being a member of a victim's family as well as an offender's family. But he only recently has come into the open with his story, which is still hard for him to talk about.

I met Sam at the pilgrimage meeting on Friday, and saw him again at Marie's workshop. When he learned I was a writer, he almost ran away like a frightened child. But after a few minutes he grew more comfortable and, since there were still a few hours left before the big awards banquet, we went downstairs to the hotel bar and talked.

"My dad was tried and convicted by the newspapers in Cleveland," Sam said, which explained his early behavior toward me. "My dad was a prominent person, and it was a very ugly murder. My mother was pregnant. The place was wiped clean, and the police couldn't find a suspect. The editor of the Cleveland Press literally decided that my father was the culprit and was being protected. He went after him with the newspaper 'to protect the community.' But I never doubted my dad was innocent."

Sam said his experience tore the rest of his family apart. This is why he formed Families of Murder Victims Against the Death Penalty, not only to show that not all members of murder victims' families are pro-death penalty, but also to keep these fragile family relationships from coming undone.

"People who are being executed today have sons and daughters, and I predict these sons and daughters will get into drug abuse, homelessness or mental institutions very quickly," Sam said. "These tragedies create other tragedies. They blow up families on both sides of the issue.

"I have seen both sides, so I think I can mediate between the two. In regard to the loss and grieving they go through, the families of the victim and the offender are similar."

I told Sam about Patti Linebaugh, and asked what he would tell someone like her who supports the death penalty.

"I would not try to change her mind, but rather get her some help to cope with her pain. Not to change her mind, but to help her."

Sam excused himself to go back to his room and change for the banquet. I was already wearing a jacket and tie, so I decided to wait out the next hour or so in the bar to review my notes, and wonder what would happen next.

The ballroom was packed — wall to wall abolitionists, from D.C. Council members to November West. The gang was all here. I had a great table, though it was purely by chance. Next to me was Michael Millman, head of the California Appellate Project, which acts as a clearing house for Death Row appeals. We were joined by Henry Schwarzschild, and Mr. and Mrs. Hugo Bedau.

This was to be an evening of congratulation for some jobs well done. Marie Deans and Joe Ingle were going to be honored for their tireless work, and the Rev. Joseph Lowery was to wow the crowd with his oratory. I had yet to meet Joe. I didn't want to bother him during dinner, so I instead planned to corner him after the banquet and earn his blessing for a trip to Tennessee's Death Row.

Marie was chosen to accept her Abolitionist of the Year Award first. But before coming to the podium to give her acceptance speech, her son, Robert, had a surprise. It was a poem, written by Robert, about Marie's family both inside and outside Death Row.

We are your sons, your daughters, your sisters and your brothers. We are your clients, your hassles, your problems and your worries. We are your friends, your comrades, your roommates and your strugglemates.

To you, we are all this, and more. But to them, and to me, you will always be, Saint Marie."

Marie looked completely shocked as she moved toward the podium to accept the award and a hug from her son. The moment obviously gave her a huge lift, and her speech gushed with optimism.

"My grandmother used to tell me that it was always dark before the dawn, and I think it's getting real dark, and I think there's a dawn out there," she said. "I think we can do this in a lot shorter time than we've been talking about. It's out there for us, the country is beginning to turn. I truly think Joe Ingle and I are going to outlive the death penalty.

"I want to thank all of you, and I want you to know that you are my family. There's some hard times in 18 years of this, and we in the South feel isolated most of the time. It's hard to go down to the death house, it's hard to watch them be killed. They're guys you've come to love, even if you don't like them."

She then ended her comments in true Marie Deans fashion. "Let's get rid of this damn thing."

Next it was Joe's turn. He mustered a weak smile as his accolades were read back to him: nominated for the Nobel Peace Prize in 1988 and 1989; founder and director of the Southern Coalition on Jails and Prisons; minister to more than 400 men sentenced to death in the Southern United States.

I say mustered a smile because he looked ragged, as if he were completely preoccupied and simply wanted to be somewhere else. As it turned out, I was right.

"Even as a I stand up here tonight, my joy is tempered because I have a dear friend, a man who is on Death Row in Florida State Prison by the name of Ray Clark, who has been there since 1977, and who is set for execution Nov. 14," Joe told the hushed gathering. "I've been visiting Ray for years, and there is not going to be any clemency in this case. Ray knows he is going to be executed.

"But my wife, Becca, and I have won this trip to Paris, and we are leaving at 5 p.m. tomorrow afternoon. We're real excited about this, but I'm also aware of the fact that I'm going to be in Paris on Nov. 14. Ray Clark is going to be in Florida State Prison. As Ray and I have exchanged letters, and realized this was real, we decided to set up a phone call. I think the story of this phone call is, in a little way, the story of why we are all here tonight.

"Here is a man I have visited since 1977, a man who I have loved like a brother. I am going to be out of the country, and we asked the prison to arrange one final phone call with Ray and me tomorrow, before I get on the plane to Paris. The Florida State Prison refused that request.

"What is at the heart of this essentially evil thing...," Joe, visibly moved, paused to compose himself. "The inability to regard other people as human beings. To disregard their feelings completely, to objectify them so you can exterminate them. That's what they're doing with Ray, and that's what they're doing to me.

"The challenge is not to let that contaminate you," he said. "Because I have learned love from people like Ray Clark, I have been able to love back. There are human beings in there who are loved and loving.

"I know the work we have done together through the years is united by a bond between the living and the dead. It is a bond that runs through this room tonight, amongst us and through us. This line that has formed is coming into a circle — and when it concludes, we'll be able to look back at the heartache and the pain, and the lost lives, the evil of it all, the love we've shared, and know that we have triumphed. I hope that you will remember that, and as we leave here, we will march into the future together."

I thought about Joe's words, and his dilemma, for the rest of the banquet. Even while Dr. Lowery spoke so eloquently on the death penalty and his relationship with Martin Luther King Jr., I thought about Joe Ingle and Ray Clark. And I realized that purely by coincidence, I was going to be in Florida for Ray's execution. Not Joe, but me.

I didn't mention this to Joe when I finally met him after the banquet. Once he had a chance to size me up, he agreed to meet me in Tennessee in a few weeks and take me to Death Row. I wanted to talk to him some more, but we kept getting interrupted by well-wishers offering congratulations. Finally, it was Marie who broke off our discussion.

"We just won an award," she screamed at Joe. "We have to go drink!"

Sunday was Veterans' Day, a fact I nearly overlooked as I packed my belongings — this time I stayed in a hotel — and prepared for a morning at the Howard Inn and an afternoon of driving to Virginia for my interview with Joe Giarratano.

There was one more workshop, this one dealing with those who were victims of the death penalty. The speaker was Bob Doemer, the man from the Friday pilgrimage reunion meeting who spent "17 months, 26 days, 8 hours and 10 minutes" on Death Row more than 25 years ago. He was big and burly, with a used car salesman's taste in clothes, and a warm personality,

Bob, who described himself as "both a victim and a survivor," had his sentence reversed by the U.S. Supreme Court, and he was acquitted in a subsequent trial after his innocence was proved beyond a reasonable doubt. It turned out that the alleged victim in the case actually died of natural causes.

"For me and my family, it was the saddest, most miserable, and darkest hours of our lives, not knowing when, how or even if I would survive," Bob said of his time on Death Row. "I didn't know whether I would see another sunset, or touch those that I love the most. My business went bankrupt, we lost our home, we

"We Shall Overcome" —the final moments of the 1990 National Coalition to Abolish the Death Penalty's conference, Washington D.C.

had to liquidate every asset that I had. My wife had to go to work to support herself and our two daughters.

"The quiet on Death Row was almost unnerving," he said. "It was like living in a bathroom — and of course, we didn't have a key to the door.

"While on the Row, I made a promise that if God returned me to my family, I would dedicate my life to ending capital punishment. I will do that as long as God gives me breath." Bob said he almost didn't get the chance.

"My execution was stayed about three weeks before I was to go to the chair," he said. "I figured, if this is God's will, it's God's will. You become fatalistic in that situation."

Robert Bryan, head of the coalition, then came to the podium to make some closing remarks and officially end the conference. Except there was one problem: no one wanted to leave.

It started with a lone voice from the back of the ballroom, singing the opening strains of "We Shall Overcome." Soon more voices joined in, and before we knew what was happening, the entire crowd of more than 500 had clasped hands and formed a circle. The singing went on for more than 10 minutes, and when it was over, hugs and kisses were everywhere. Every last person was filled with optimism and joy.

Every person, that is, except for November West. She was crying. Alone.

"My own family abandoned me," she said through a steady stream of tears. "This is my real family."

November and I exchanged phone numbers, and after saying a couple more good-byes, I found myself outside the Howard Inn with the afternoon in front of me. I didn't have to be in Virginia until the next day, so I decided to relax and experience Washington on a bona fide national holiday. Not wanting to venture too far, I went across the street to McDonald's, bought a Sunday *Washington Post* and caught up with the outside world.

Nearby, a couple with a young child were carefully counting their dollar bills and change at an otherwise empty table. The man at the table then got up, and stood by the entrance. When I walked out, he stopped me and asked if I could spare some change. I gave him the quarters from my pocket, and went on my way.

As I got into my car, I looked back toward the McDonald's and saw the family eating hamburgers and fries. At the very least, people should be able to afford a Big Mac and fries. Especially on Veterans Day, I thought. Especially in America.

I parked at the Supreme Court building and, seeing how it was such a nice day, I decided to walk the handful of miles from the Supreme Court to the Lincoln Memorial at the end of the famed Washington Mall.

Images of America past and present appeared before my eyes: The Hare Krishnas chanting their hymns accompanied by portable synthesizers; yuppies playing touch football on the grass; the black man and white woman holding hands while reading the Emancipation Proclamation on the side of the Lincoln Memorial; the granite Vietnam Veterans Memorial, with its colorful wreaths and somber vets; and the American flag over the Capitol dome slowly, carefully being lowered with the setting sun.

This is my family, I said to myself as I drove off toward Virginia. This is my home.

CHAPTER 3
THE SAINT AND THE SINNER

"If you look at the evidence with Joe, his guilt is pretty conclusive. There is no new evidence, just old evidence in a new wrapper."

—Bert Rohrer, spokesman for the Virginia Attorney General's office.

"...I shouldn't be here. That's the bottom line."

— Joe Giarratano, Virginia Death Row inmate.

After spending nearly an hour trying to find the right highway, I finally crossed the Potomac and headed toward Richmond, the capital of the Confederacy and my first Southern stop.

I drove for hours on lonely stretches of two-lane road. This is the South, I thought. This is where people are named Billy Bob; this is where police officers wear big hats and are called "troopers"; this is where "You all" is one word, where grits are considered a breakfast staple.

Virginia had never entered my mind when I thought about going to the South. The South to me was Florida, Alabama, and Georgia. Virginia was more like a suburb of Washington, D.C. I was stopping here for one simple reason — Joe Giarratano.

I first read about Joe in *People Magazine*. He had been in many other publications previously, including the omnipresent *USA Today*. Many people knew about Joe Giarratano: from those who thought he should live, to those who wanted him to die.

I had his story committed to memory. A longshoreman from the port city of Norfolk, Joe woke from a drug-induced blackout one morning in 1979 to find his roommates, 44-year-old Barbara Kline and her 15-year-old daughter, Michelle, beaten and dead on the bathroom floor. He didn't recall the murder, but assumed his own guilt. The next day, Joe surrendered to authorities and made five separate confessions to the grisly crime.

He was convicted in a brief, non-jury trial. The judge had no problem giving Giarratano a death sentence because Joe *asked* for it. But several years later, after Joe was convinced by Marie Deans to pursue his appeals, evidence surfaced that was never addressed by the trial court.

Footprints and pubic hairs found at the scene didn't match Joe's. Barbara Kline was stabbed by a right-handed person; Joe is left-handed. Michelle was strangled with a chain necklace; in one of his confessions, Joe said he used his hands.

In the meantime, Joe was born again — not as a Christian, but as a jail house lawyer who gave up drugs and death wishes for the intoxicating power of law. He has worked on several death penalty cases, including his own, and has been published in the *Yale Law Journal* and other prestigious legal reviews.

Joe claimed his past suicidal tendencies prevented him from assisting in his own defense and that the new evidence demanded his case be heard again at the trial court level. But Virginia has strict rules regarding procedural default, making it virtually impossible for new trials to be granted simply because of apparent prior error. Nevertheless, with the help of Marie and M*A*S*H star Mike Farrell, support to win Joe a new trial poured in from all political fronts. He garnered the backing of Hollywood liberals and East Coast conservatives like columnist James Kilpatrick.

Joe's supporters, even the pro-death penalty Kilpatrick, don't seem to care that he was a drug addict and an alcoholic with a long criminal record. They don't care that he is to many Americans the epitome of evil. He may indeed be all those things and more — he just may not be a killer.

"I spent hours reading the record and came away deeply troubled," Kilpatrick wrote in one of his columns. "I am not sure that Joe is guilty; I am not sure he is innocent, but I have spent

50 years covering courts and I am certain of this: he was not convicted beyond a reasonable doubt.

"The confused, suicidal drug addict of 1979 is gone," he continued. "In his place one finds a young man with a good mind and a healthy outlook on life. How would killing him avenge the victims or sustain respect for judicial process?"

That's the question Kilpatrick and many others had asked the state of Virginia repeatedly, a request that always fell on deaf ears. Former Governor Douglas Wilder, a conservative Southern Democrat, supports the death penalty both personally and, most importantly, politically. Granting clemency to Death Row inmates can come back to haunt politicians; it helped cost former California Gov. Edmund G. "Pat" Brown his job.

But on Feb. 19, 1991, the impossible happened. Wilder, apparently tired of the mailman's constant visits and the pleas from Joe's supporters, commuted Joe's sentence to life with the possibility of parole in 2004. The commutation came just 82 hours before Joe was to die in the state's electric chair. Not a terribly close call, but close enough for Joe.

The commutation was a major milestone, though still only a half-victory; Virginia wouldn't give Joe a new trial. The state's attorney general, a scrappy, nuts-and-bolts lawyer named Mary Sue Terry, said the question of Joe's innocence had been answered.

"Mr. Giarratano has received the benefit of exhaustive legal review, and I am convinced Mr. Giarratano committed the crimes," she said in a statement the day after clemency was announced. "He is not entitled to a new trial."

According to the NAACP Legal Defense Fund, at least 1,078 Death Row inmates have had their convictions reversed since executions resumed in 1977. Of those, 27 were freed because they eventually were proven innocent. Joe is still waiting.

I met Joe three months before his sentence was commuted, back when death was a very real possibility. And since I didn't have the benefit of hindsight while driving to Richmond, all I knew then was that I was going to meet a somewhat famous Death Row inmate, and that I was fairly nervous.

I couldn't get my mind off him. I tried, but there wasn't much on the highway to distract my thoughts. I contemplated our upcoming interview and how I possibly could get him to say or reveal something he hadn't already told the hundreds of other reporters who have come his way. I wondered whether I would believe his story like so many others had, whether I would be taken in by his charm or be repulsed.

By the time I returned from my silent deliberations, night had descended and I was in Richmond. I couldn't see much in the dark, but I would have tomorrow to explore and learn more about Joe Giarratano. I found a Super 8 motel, ate at a local diner and went back to my room to stare at the ceiling, with the TV emoting in the background. I did this until midnight, when my eyes finally decided it was time for a rest.

I awoke to the sound of big-rig trucks and the television set. It was only a 10-minute drive to downtown and the Capitol, where I was to attend a press conference, and I still had plenty of time to spare. I decided to get an early start and do some sightseeing.

Richmond looks much like any other large city. There are lots of buildings crammed together, a major university, museums, department stores and an occasional patch of grass. I kept thinking that this didn't look like the South, but then I didn't really know what the South was supposed to look like.

Locating the Capitol complex was my first goal. Drawing from what I knew about Sacramento and Missouri, I figured it wouldn't be hard to miss a large, domed building, even in a big city. Not hard, that is, provided the Capitol has a dome — and Richmond's doesn't. I discovered that rather important stylistic difference after driving past the Capitol building, twice.

Humble is the best way to describe the Virginia State Capitol. It's small but stately, looking more like a quaint mansion than an edifice of government, except for the telltale Roman pillars. Tara it wasn't, but it was close. It had style. Rolling green hills surrounded it and statues of George Washington were everywhere — though the building was designed by Thomas Jefferson. It looked like a great place for a family picnic. And if you sit in just the right spot, you can gaze down the street and see the cold, gray building that houses the state's electric chair.

The press conference was in House Room #5, on the fourth floor. Camera crews worked feverishly to set up just the right angle. Reporters milled about, peeking at the table of literature about Joe, his case, and the death penalty. I felt strangely at home with all these reporters, yet uncomfortable at the same time. I was glad I wasn't one of them — and I was jealous.

Marie was there, standing behind a table with petitions signed by more than 15,000 people from the United States and around the world, all asking Governor Wilder for clemency and a new trial on Joe's behalf. And there was Mike Farrell, looking every bit his B.J. Hunnicutt character with that soft smile and those caring blue eyes.

Mike Farrell at a press conference on behalf of Joe Giarratano, Virginia State Capitol, Richmond

The irony was too strong to miss. Farrell was here to do what he could to help Joe, but the press was here to see Farrell. Joe may be news, but Farrell still got the top billing.

I took a seat in the corner, partly to stay out of the way and partly to take in the scene. Marie and a few others spoke briefly about Joe and the petitions, and about how they were going to deliver the signatures to Wilder's office after the press conference. Few of the reporters paid much attention.

Then it was Farrell's turn. On went the lights and tape recorders. Now the show could begin.

"This case describes for thousands of people around the world that fairness is being lost, and that individuals and truth are being gobbled up in a system that has become creaky and rusty," Farrell said. "The system has lost the focus on what is significant. Individuals are what matter, and the system must be made to accommodate the needs of the individual, not the other way around.

"I find Joe Giarratano to be a simply extraordinary individual," Farrell continued. "His history provides to me the example of what is possible in terms of transformation, how one can go from one of society's throwaways to being a contributing member of society, in spite of the circumstances in which he finds himself."

Having said that, Farrell, armed with the petitions, led the faithful band of journalists through the back stairwells of Jefferson's edifice to Wilder's office. Of course, Wilder wasn't there, but an aide accepted the petitions in the governor's absence. Cameramen were jostling each other, trying to aim their video lenses into the tiny office where Farrell and the aide, executive assistant Mac McFarlane, stood.

Farrell was trying to convince McFarlane that Wilder had the political leverage to grant Joe a new trial. McFarlane respectfully disagreed.

"The governor has no power to influence the judiciary," McFarlane said. "Only the judiciary can grant a new trial."

An Associated Press reporter and I talked to McFarlane and Farrell for a few minutes, until the two men asked to be alone for a while. I went into the hall to join the rest of the pack and to collect my thoughts.

A television reporter was pacing the hallway looking for something to do. Suddenly, Marie shuffled by, but before she could get to the governor's office to tell Farrell it was time to go to the prison and visit Joe, the reporter shoved a microphone toward her face. Her eyes darted nervously across the hallway in search of an escape. There was none — she was surrounded by journalists. I was amazed to see the woman who had spoken so optimistically and forcefully in Washington become unsettled when confronted by the media. She is not shy by any means, and gives a great quote, but she prefers to keep the spotlight on her clients, the inmates of Death Row; she despises being the center of attention herself.

Marie fidgeted and grasped for excuses to leave. Finally, when her excuses fell flat, the lanky Southerner agreed to make a statement.

"I want people to know Joe is innocent, that he needs help, and that they should come to his rescue," she said shakily, squinting uncomfortably under the bright lights.

As soon as the reporter returned the microphone to his face to ask a question, Marie took advantage of the opening and made a mad dash for the governor's office. Behind me, I heard a muffled laugh.

"Saint Marie," said the voice, adding another chuckle.

I guess I turned around so fast that I drew the voice's attention. The giggly one was Esther Schmidt, who was standing with her husband, Frank. Both were freelance writers by profession, though they were here today to show support for Joe. I asked Esther about her "Saint Marie" comment, and whether people in Virginia really believed that to be true.

"Well, there are no true saints on Earth, but Marie works hard," she said. "When you work hard for something you believe in, anyone can be considered a saint."

I decided to dedicate the rest of my trip to the task of achieving sainthood. Imagine, a Jewish saint. Now that would really be something to write about.

The press event now officially over, it was time to explore the streets of Richmond. Before I left the Capitol, however, I had my freelance writer friends show me the way to the Attorney General's office. Sticking to my strategy of surprise, I thought I might try my luck and drop in on the A.G. herself, or at least a subordinate who could give an inquisitive out-of-towner a quick primer on justice, Virginia-style.

As expected, Attorney General Terry wasn't available. The downstairs security guard, however, was more than helpful, and called upstairs to see if Bert Rohrer, Terry's spokesman, could meet with me. While waiting for an answer, I asked the guard her opinion on the death penalty and the South. She seemed reticent about the whole capital punishment thing, though when pressed for a position she said, "Well, I guess if they really are brutal then maybe they should be killed."

I asked her about Florida, her home state and my next big stop, and then mentioned I would be traveling on to Georgia and Alabama.

"Alabama?" she said with alarm. "Now that's a scary place. That is one backwards state."

As it turned out, Rohrer was more than available, he was downright bored. We talked for about two hours, though much of the time I felt like I was talking to a robot cranking out the proper administrative line. Rohrer dismissed all the attention around Joe, saying that the inmate had a better public relations campaign than a case.

"If you look at the evidence with Joe, his guilt is pretty conclusive," Rohrer said. "There is no new evidence, just old evidence in a new wrapper.

"We have 140 lawyers, and death penalty cases constitute a significant portion of our work. It's something the attorney general takes very seriously. There's nothing you take more seriously than the death penalty."

We continued talking, reporter to robot, until finally it was time to leave. I turned off the tape recorder and started for the door. Then something remarkable happened. Rohrer turned into a human being. Without the tape rolling, he started to talk about the death penalty with real emotion.

I was already in the elevator when he opened up. I didn't want to scare him by taking notes, but when I got downstairs, I ran into a bathroom and wrote down every word.

"It seems that we get more serious crimes here in Virginia," Rohrer said. "In Texas, a guy was sent to death for participating in a murder-robbery at a 7-Eleven. The partner, who actually pulled the trigger, laughed as his friend was taken to be executed. Here, though, with things like Giarratano's murder of those two women... That was a heinous crime. Horrible. Just horrible."

Rohrer lowered his head. Continuing to hold open the elevator doors, he said, "Nothing is more serious than a government taking a life. The death penalty is difficult. It's not a game — it's about as serious as it can get."

For two hours, Rohrer tried to put the death penalty on a purely legal level. But his comments just before I left illustrated how little capital punishment has to do with the law.

"It's emotional," Rohrer said. "In a trial's penalty phase, it's the emotions you're appealing to; it's got nothing to do with law or justice. It's how you use emotion to invoke feelings of mercy or revenge."

I spent the rest of the afternoon walking around downtown Richmond, mingling amongst the tourists and conventioneers. I talked to some city folk about the death penalty, and found that most people had heard of the Joe Giarratano case. One guy at a Radio Shack where I went to buy more cassettes spent 30 minutes telling me how wrong the state was in not granting a new trial. He talked so much, I also bought some batteries, just so I wouldn't feel like I was loitering.

My small hotel room was a welcome sight by the end of this long and eventful day. Dinner was two tuna sandwiches and a bag of potato chips, provided by my trusty Igloo traveling kitchen.

I went to sleep that night thinking about a man some call a killer and others a victim. I wouldn't be the first reporter to meet Joe Giarratano; that didn't bother me. What disturbed me the most was that I could be the last.

The Mecklenburg Correctional Center is two hours south of Richmond near the North Carolina border. Except for the four lanes of modern highway, the demons of progress had by-passed much of this part of the country. Trees lined each side of Interstate 85, and at the interchange with U.S. 58, the trees made room for small communities of rickety houses, churches and auto shops. A sign near a roadside cemetery proclaimed, "You will be born again."

Crossing a bridge, I could see the faint outline of barbed wire fences. A lone tower stood on the horizon, peeking over a barricade of bushy trees. Another sign further down the road confirmed my suspicions.

"Dead End," it read.

This was the entrance to the prison — and Death Row. I turned into the parking lot and stopped in front of the main building, a relatively new structure that was absent the drab aura one usually associates with prison architecture. Some secretaries were power walking around the grounds, stomping past circles of barbed wire perched atop an electrified fence.

I was early, so I decided to take some pictures before going inside. I only clicked off a few frames, however, before a rather unhappy-looking guard came from nowhere to inquire, as politely as he could, just what the hell I was doing.

He was abrasive at first, but then I did what I always do when confronted by authority: I groveled. Somehow, I switched the subject to the weather, and how awfully nice it was in Virginia for being so close to Christmas. Realizing that I was harmless, he led me to the reception area and went on his merry way.

After signing in and submitting to a routine search, I was escorted to the capital punishment wing by a female guard who, among her other duties, was the Row's law librarian. She knew Joe well, perhaps better than any other guard, and even went to him on many occasions to seek legal advice for herself.

"I didn't know Joe when he first got here, so it's hard for me to say what his original personality was," she told me. "But he's a great hand at legal matters. He's a great help for setting me and others on the right track for finding legal materials.

"I find him to be no different than any other man," she said, reaching for one of her many keys. "He's an all around average Joe." We proceeded through a heavy metal door and turned a corner. My eyes fell onto Joe's bearded, smiling face as the door slammed shut.

If Joe Giarratano is an animal, as many death penalty supporters believe him to be, then he is a teddy bear. He laughed and joked with the guards, his robust belly and boisterous disposition seemed more suited to a department store Santa Claus than

Joe Giarratano, Mecklenburg Correctional Center, Virginia

a convict. Only his light blue prison work shirt and handcuffs served notice to his dire straits.

We walked into a small, wood-paneled room with just enough space for a table, two ashtrays and a couple of plastic chairs. There were glass windows all around, and a disinterested guard sat about 50 feet away.

Joe switched on a small air conditioner in the corner, and maneuvered his burly longshoreman hands to light a cigarette. He drew it to his lips, exposing a tattoo on his woolly forearm.

"It means 'Stand alone against the world'," Joe said, noticing my stare. "It's something I think all of us have to do at one point or another...to discover who we are."

I reminded Joe that he wasn't alone, and that if he hadn't discovered that himself by now, he must not read the papers or watch the news. What he is, I suggested politely, is a celebrity. And politely, he agreed.

"It pleases me that people are taking an interest, but on a higher level, it's people who wouldn't normally take an interest in a death penalty case or the issue," he said. "With the current political atmosphere around the death penalty, it's really surprising that people are taking such notice and concern.

"I mean, I made an impact on James Kilpatrick," he added, a feat he relishes telling. "I don't think he'll look at the death penalty the same way again...I think that about a lot of people."

Pursuing the political angle, Joe said he hoped Wilder eventually will share Kilpatrick's feelings and push for a new trial.

"I think Governor Wilder is a fair man. If he sits down and really looks at the case...he's in the position of authority where he can assure I'll get a new trial. If I'm found innocent, he's clear. And if I'm found guilty, he's clear.

"I guess on one level my situation has been helpful, because it has brought attention to how the death penalty works in Virginia, and the big issue in Virginia which is procedural default. Virginia has the toughest procedural default rules in the country."

Suddenly, I was no longer talking to a convicted murderer. I was in law school, listening to a lecture from John Houseman.

The uppity, eastern accent may have been replaced by a Southern twang, but the intensity of the message was the same. Joe appeared more articulate than some governors I've met, and he's probably better versed in the law, too.

Joe explained that procedural default can have several interpretations, though it generally means that issues not raised at the trial level cannot be reintroduced on subsequent appeals. In Joe's case, he and his lawyers claim there is new evidence valid enough to warrant a new trial, not simply a new appeal. Joe wore a cold stare while being reminded of the bureaucracy stacked against him. This drug addict turned jailhouse lawyer craves justice, and while he talked of casework and becoming a real lawyer someday, he also berated those in his newfound profession who have abandoned him — and abandoned the truth.

"The state knows. The prosecutor and the world knows that a mistake has been made," Joe said. "It's simply politics, because nobody wants to accept responsibility. It's not the system so much that's screwed up, but the people that run the system. Our adversarial system doesn't have anything to do with finding truth, and it doesn't have anything to do with seeking justice. It's a contest of who can get the best lawyer and win.

"I haven't asked to be set free," he continued. "What I've asked for is a new trial, which I think if I'm given, I'll be acquitted."

Our conversation soon turned from the problems of the present to those of the past. Joe's childhood, I learned, was not one to be envied. His long road to Death Row began as an offspring of Florida's lucrative drug trade. His stepfather was a junkie and his mother was a dealer. Young Joe, along with his two younger sisters and one younger brother, was born into a brutish world of beatings, sexual abuse, and broken dreams.

"I didn't have a life," he said matter-of-factly. "I was a drug addict. I grew up around the criminal element and drugs."

He started using morphine and Demerol when he was 10 years old. Then Quaaludes, amphetamines, and any other pill he could get his hands on. Drugs were a way of escaping from reality and deadening the pain of his surroundings. It got worse.

He tried to commit suicide several times. He wound up in mental hospitals, then reform school. He met his natural father for the first and only time while serving a sentence in an adult prison. Joe's father was a junkie, too; they never spoke to each other, though at that time they seemed to have a lot in common. When Joe returned home, he helped his mother run drugs. He was all but washed up before he was old enough to vote.

In 1976, he fled his destructive home environment in Florida and came to the Virginia coast to work on the fishing boats. Joe told me he couldn't remember a day while living in Norfolk when he wasn't high on drugs. But the high life came crashing down in 1979 when he discovered Barbara and Michelle Kline's dead bodies. He said he assumed his own guilt in a desperate attempt to end his pain.

"My only interest then was I wanted to die, and here was a way to do it," he said. "That's the only thing that hit me, that death was the way to end everything. And if I couldn't do it myself, then the state would do it for me."

He tried to do it himself several times during his brief trial. Finally, based on Joe's confessions and his overwhelming desire to be punished — he wouldn't let his lawyer plea bargain for a lesser sentence — the judge granted Joe's death wish.

"I asked for it. I begged for the death penalty," Joe said. "I wrote the judge. I said, 'Hey judge, kill me, I'm evil. I'm evil to the core.'"

Joe continued to believe that until one day in 1983, when, just hours before the state was about to carry out his sentence, Marie Deans stomped into his life. Joe, who had dropped his appeals, told her the same things he had been telling everyone else who was trying to save him — that he deserved to die.

Marie didn't buy it.

"She told me I was full of shit," Joe said. "Here's this big, macho convict sitting down here in this room, and here's this woman, this total stranger telling me I'm full of shit. She said I was copping out, I wasn't accepting responsibility for who I was, I wasn't accepting responsibility for what I did, I wasn't accepting responsibility for anything. She said I wanted to cop out and that I was a coward. Well, that got my attention.

"She just sat there and told me, 'You are not evil, you are a human being and you are a worthy human being.' Everybody before had supported my decision, that I was evil and that I was sick, and that I was the devil and needed to be put out of my misery."

What followed — after Marie convinced Joe to pick up his appeals — was hours of counseling and self-motivated rehabilitation. And as the new evidence suggesting his innocence came to light, so did a new Joe Giarratano.

It was a remarkable transformation. He plunged himself into the law, becoming a dedicated student and eventually a teacher. He prepared cases on behalf of other Death Row inmates, one of which was argued before the U.S. Supreme Court. Death Row, Joe said, saved his life.

"There's no doubt in my mind I would have been dead within a matter of months anyway before coming here," he said. "At the time of my arrest I was jaundiced, my liver was shot. They described me as a walking toxic waste dump. How long could I have gone on like that? I've lived more here in the last six years than I ever lived before."

Looking at him and talking to him, I could see why he has been able to change the way many people look at capital punishment. If capital punishment changed him, it was for the better.

"I don't think any prison in this country is conducive to rehabilitation," Joe said. "A person has to want to change, and you have to have a reason to change. Marie pushed me into the law as a way of helping 'her', so I felt obligated. Once I got involved in that, I saw it as a way to get back at these sons-of-bitches at the prison and in Richmond.

"But as I read more and learned more, it got me to thinking. I read old Supreme Court cases, I got into poetry and a whole different world of ideas, and being isolated and having the time to be with myself helped. Since then, my world has never been limited. I grew up.

"I don't care if people don't believe that I've changed," he continued, his cigarette burning down to his fingers. "The fact is that I'm innocent, and all I want is for the evidence to be heard. I don't think the average person is concerned about whether I've changed; that's not the issue. If I'm innocent, then I shouldn't be here. That's the bottom line."

Joe and I talked for a little more than two hours, about the death penalty and everything and anything in between. And the more we talked, the more I grew to like him. If not for the handcuffs, I never would have known he was an inmate. Whenever I caught myself staring at the cuffs, I immediately moved my eyes down to his spanking new, Nike high-top athletic shoes. He was hardly a basketball player, but they looked good on him anyway.

Joe puts people at ease. His self-education is remarkable; when we talked, he used legal terminology to rival the most experienced of lawyers. He was bright, at times witty, and most of all, human. He was always human.

I'm still not sure Joe is innocent, and I'm not even sure if a new trial would convince me. But I do know this: Joe Giarratano is not the crazed psychotic who arrived on Virginia's Death Row in 1979. He not only has metamorphosed into a different person, he already has made a positive difference in the world. Looking back, it didn't take compassion for Governor Wilder to spare Joe's life — only common sense.

I would like to have stayed longer with Joe and gotten to know him better, but my time was up and he had to go back to his cell. He may be a celebrity to the world, but in prison he's just another inmate.

Joe and I shook hands and promised to stay in touch. I watched as he was led upstairs to his unit with his head down. I wondered if I would ever see him again. I hoped I would get that chance.

A different guard was to be my escort out of the prison and back to reality. He was a tall, wiry African-American who had a pleasant disposition for someone faced with working on Death

Row. As we left the unit, inmates behind far-off windows called his name, and the guard answered back with a wave and a smile.

One inmate, obviously referring to me, inquired, "Is that guy a lawyer?"

"No," my escort replied. "He's a writer here to see Joe."

Joe, I quickly learned during our five-minute walk, was one of this guard's favorite subjects. He told me with excitement in his voice how television crews from "20/20" and "Inside Edition" had been to the prison to see Joe, and he gushed about the previous day when Farrell paid his visit.

"If Joe gets a new trial, I think he'll have a chance," the guard said, rubbing his chin. "Everybody here respects him."

The guard didn't want to be quoted by name, but I took down his words anyway. His honesty was not something you get very often.

"I've worked Death Row for two years," he said, standing at the gate separating us from the outside world. "When you work with them you just work, you try not to get involved, because once you get to know them you find out they're human beings just like us.

"They don't give us no problems," he said before sending me on my way. "We just do our work, and they just do theirs. They just try to get off of that Death Row."

It was near dusk now, and though I had no real schedule, I felt I needed to get on my way to Florida. This usually was the time, right before a long drive, that I would plop in a tape and sing along. But for almost three hours, I drove in silence. All I heard was the clanging of prison bars and the hum of the road.

Eventually, it was time to fuel my car as well as my body. I was in North Carolina now, a new state for me, and I took a second to ponder North Carolina's significance. All I could come up with was Jesse Helms and tobacco. What a deadly combination.

During dinner, I read a story in the local paper about a 57-year-old woman, Blanche Taylor Moore, who was faced with either life in prison without parole or execution. She was found guilty of poisoning her former boyfriend, Raymond Reid, and now the county prosecutor wanted the jury to give her death.

Prosecutor Janet Branch not only used emotion to get Moore executed, she used the Bible. Reading from the sacred book and standing in front of Moore, Branch said: "A lying tongue...hands that shed innocent blood...a heart that deviseth wicked imaginations...feet that be swift and running to mischief...a false witness that speaketh lies."

She sure laid it on thick. After snapping the Bible shut in Moore's face, Branch said: "The law was made to put a woman like her to death."

Interesting strategy, I thought, to use a Bible to kill someone. This, of course, *was* the Bible Belt. Out here, it seems that belief in the death penalty and belief in God are one and the same. I have never met a fervent death penalty supporter who didn't also have an equally fervent or greater faith in the Lord. The ultimate punishment sanctioned by the ultimate authority.

During closing arguments, Branch's voice cracked and she cried. The jury was in the palms of her hands.

"We'd be deader than doornails if it would serve her purpose," Branch said. "This is a great honor to you and yours, when you make her pay with her life."

The jury's decision was easy. Moore was a killer, a murdering monster. They voted to kill.

I drove on, down to South Carolina where I would spend the night before heading to Florida. From Interstate 95 I found Florence, a quaint town with more lights and activity than I had encountered in many miles. I took a detour through downtown Florence before checking into the local Holiday Inn. Gazing at the tree-lined streets draped with Christmas lights made me forget about the death penalty, at least for a little bit.

Friday, November 16, started out great and quickly turned horrible. The horror began when I called Susan Cary, a Florida capital punishment lawyer who had been trying to set up interviews for me with some Death Row inmates. She got three people to agree, and all I had to do was call the prison and tell them I was coming. Well, when the prison officials asked if I were currently employed by a news organization, I did something I shouldn't have — I told the truth.

Bad move. Although I had a valid press pass, I didn't have a valid job. The interviews were off.

I called Susan to see if she could help, but no luck. It was out of her hands. I called the prison back to see if I at least could set up an interview with the warden. He was out of town for the upcoming Thanksgiving holiday. I asked the secretary if I could speak to his assistants, but she responded, with more than a hint of arrogance, "Neither of them would really want to do that."

I hated Florida.

After being transferred all over the place, I finally got the assistant secretary of prison operations, or something like that. He said Bob MacMaster, the head press flak, probably would be available. Great — from three inmates to a flak. That's like going to a five-star restaurant and discovering all they have left are grilled cheese sandwiches and french fries. Of course, I would have to eat what was on my plate. I really didn't have any other choice.

Besides, I probably couldn't have picked a more interesting weekend to be in Florida, at least for my purposes. The next afternoon, Raymond Clark was set to die in the electric chair at the state prison in Starke.

For most people, Florida means Anita Bryant, spring break and Disneyworld. For me, it meant death, plain and simple. I feared the state since my senior year of college. During the time I was covering Missouri's first execution in 23 years, Florida was celebrating its umpteenth electrocution, this one of a man named Ted Bundy.

People didn't usually make a fuss over executions, but Bundy was different. He was one of us. He was white and well educated. He looked like the boy next door, the kind who never kisses on the first date and calls everyone's parents "sir" and "ma'am".

But he also killed — at least two women, raped and murdered. He later confessed to more than 20 killings, appalling Floridians and capturing the attention of the rest of the country as well. If he was black we could understand. If he was poor, well, that was a reason. But Bundy was none of those things. In the minds of the public at large, he had betrayed his own kind.

So his execution was turned into a celebration, as Dan Horowitz so clearly described at the pilgrimage meeting in Washington. Thousands lined the road in front of the prison, many wearing "Bye Bye Bundy" t-shirts. The national media, of course, was out in full force, reporting and photographing the morbid mayhem with tabloid-style persistence. Police officers, sworn to uphold the law and be examples for others to follow, cheered and danced at Bundy's demise; barbecues were held in his honor, called "Bundy-cues".

I felt like the only person on Earth who saw the display as utterly disgusting. Supporting Bundy's execution was one thing, but celebrating and rejoicing in it was entirely another matter. I wrote an editorial for the school newspaper about how horrible the scene was, and how we all should be repulsed by the actions of our Southern neighbor. But few, it seemed, read it, and those that did, didn't care. Bundy was a 20th-Century Judas, and this time he was going to pay.

That was my first encounter with Florida justice. It was enough, however, to convince me that I couldn't fully experience the effect of the death penalty in the United States without experiencing Florida. Little did I know how real my experience would be.

I didn't plan on being in Florida for an execution, just as I'm sure Joe Ingle didn't plan on going to Paris for Ray Clark's final hours. But I was here, and Joe was there. I felt sorry for Joe, and I felt sorry for Ray, too. But Ray Clark was still just a name. Because of that, it was difficult for me to focus my concern. I tried, but all I could think about was what a perfect time this was to talk to Floridians about the death penalty. I hated myself for feeling lucky — after all, a man was going to die. From a writer's point of view, it was a scene I couldn't have set better myself.

So, eager to continue this compelling yet repelling journey, I packed my tribulations into the Acura and sped toward the state of sunshine, oranges, and one of America's most active execution chambers.

That myth about "southern hospitality" turns out to be true. People are so friendly down here it's actually sort of unnerving. Friendly and religious, I might add. My waitress at a South Carolina Shoney's was wearing a "Jesus Loves You" pin, and on the back of my check she wrote, "God Bless You."

An elderly woman at the same restaurant, who was taking a seat in nearby booth, stopped at my table, said "praise the Lord," and handed me a pamphlet on Christianity titled "Christmas Greetings".

About 50 miles from the Florida border, I heard a song titled "Rotting on Demand," about an innocent man sentenced to prison. "This isn't a court of justice, son," the song says. "This is a court of law."

Entering Florida, right before the St. Mary's River, a tiny band of palm trees stood silent watch. I left the main highway and connected with a two-lane road that would take me to Gainesville, my stop for the night. It's not that I was trying to avoid the prison; I just wanted to wait until the sun came up before facing an actual execution — I felt I could deal with Starke much better in the light. Besides, Gainesville was a college town with a lot of hotels and, for all I knew, Starke had nothing more than a filling station.

It was late, and I was getting tired. I wanted to rest before the next day's execution. I rolled down a window to keep myself awake, an old technique, but effective. My nose suddenly picked up an odd odor. It smelled like something was burning, maybe a fireplace, or a barbecue. I thought it could very well be the sunset; the sun, shrouded by gray clouds, didn't really go down. It just kind of smoldered into the night.

I looked up. A dim sign flickered a message into the starless sky. "Welcome to Starke."

CHAPTER 4
ELECTRIC JUSTICE

"It's just a hollow victory. Nothing will bring him back."
— Regina M. Sheridan, after her husband's murderer was made eligible for the death penalty.

"They're on him now."
— Death penalty supporter, shortly after the execution of Ray Clark had begun.

The Florida Department of Corrections couldn't have asked for a better day to execute Ray Clark.

The sun beamed through a cloudless sky, bathing Gainesville in 70 degrees of humidified perfection. Thousands of football fans were preparing to watch the University of Florida Gators take on the Kentucky Wildcats. Life this Saturday carried on unobstructed and uninhibited as I drove back along state Highway 26, toward U.S. 301 and the tiny — and as I learned the previous night, very nearby — hamlet of Starke. College students, parents, grandparents and children were out and about, laughing and smiling. At the same time, nearly a world away, President George Bush was delivering a speech in Czechoslovakia to commemorate the Velvet Revolution, which swept former political prisoner Vaclav Havel to the presidency. Bush talked a lot about freedom, and how Czechoslovakia could, and should, let its freedom bells ring.

Thirty miles in front of me, a bell of a different kind was tolling for Ray Clark. In six hours, he would be dead.

When I arrived at my hotel Friday night, I bought every newspaper I could find in the hopes of learning something, anything about Ray Clark. The *Gainesville Sun* had two stories about Death Row, though not about Clark specifically. One was about Roy Clifton Swafford, who just the day before had come within two hours of being executed on his first death warrant. Swafford, convicted of a 1982 rape and murder of a service station clerk, had shared his "last meal" with Ray.

That last-meal thing has always amazed me. The one bit of freedom prisoners are granted is the choice of what they want to eat before death, as if it really matters at that point. If it were me, I would ask for a bucket of salt-water taffy and a pack of gum.

The other story was about Ronald Palmer Heath, a 29-year-old who had been found guilty of robbing and murdering a Gainesville businessman in 1989. Heath's brother, Kenny, actually shot the man, Michael J. Sheridan, but plea bargained and received a life sentence in exchange for testifying against his brother. As a result, Ronald, who slit Sheridan's throat, was now eligible for the death penalty.

Kenny Heath said he was just following his brother's orders, the classic Nuremburg defense. The businessman's family, however, didn't seem to care who was responsible for the murder. Unlike the vengeful crime victims that prosecutors like the public to see, the Sheridan family was more concerned with the heart of the matter — their dead relative.

"It's just a hollow victory," Regina M. Sheridan, the victim's wife of six years, said after the guilty verdict. "Nothing will bring him back." So very true. But sorry, Regina, in Florida you cannot finish mourning your husband's death until Heath dies as well.

I had hoped to learn more about Ray from Susan Cary, my Death Row contact who had set up the interviews for me, but she was extremely hard to get on the phone. I felt that I needed to talk to her, not just because of Ray, but because she is more than just a lawyer. She, like Joe Ingle, is there with the inmates until they die. What stories she could tell, I thought.

But not last night. Her unanswered home telephone probably meant she was at the prison, holding Ray's hand or doing whatever it is she does to help the condemned cope with death.

I couldn't help but feel like a vulture, intruding into a world where I didn't belong. I quit my job to take this journey, but I could always go home; I could always go back to the other world. Not everyone has that luxury. Ray Clark can never go back and Susan Cary's commitment won't let her.

There was one note of optimism in the Friday papers. A Death Row inmate was granted a new sentencing hearing by the Florida Supreme Court. Of course, judging from the state's track record, his chances of getting off Death Row couldn't be viewed as terribly promising.

Ray did make the morning papers. For the first time, I was able to put a face with the name. He had long, Elvis Presley sideburns and short cropped hair that was parted in the middle. His eyes were big and wide, producing an eerie look when coupled with his square jaw and closed mouth.

The story told me what I already knew. It said that pending 11th-hour appeals, Ray would die at 6:01 p.m. tonight in the state's electric chair. This was Ray's fifth death warrant. He originally was scheduled to die earlier in the week, but his attorneys were able to get temporary stays. His future didn't look good. Only one person, Willie Darden, has ever survived a fifth death warrant in Florida.

The majority of Floridians seem to be deeply committed to their death penalty. It's woven deeply and lovingly into the fabric of Florida life. When the U.S. Supreme Court overturned the death penalty in 1972 and said states would have to rewrite their statutes to fit constitutional requirements, Florida was the first to do so. The Florida Legislature even went into special session just so it could bring the death penalty back as soon as possible.

The rest of the South quickly followed. From 1976, when the Supreme Court once again allowed death sentences to be carried out, to 1991, 108 of the 145 executions in the United States were in the South. Ray was on track to become the 25th person executed in Florida since the death penalty's reinstatement. He would be the state's 222nd electric chair victim overall.

Ray's sentence, according to newspaper accounts, was handed down after the 49-year-old inmate was convicted in September 1977 of killing David Drake, a St. Petersburg businessman. After Drake wrote a check for $5,000, Clark told him to kneel in the bushes and shot him twice in the head. It was a gruesome, horrible crime. They all are. All murder is horrible, no matter who does it, no matter how it is done.

My stomach was in knots as I approached U.S. 301, Starke's main thoroughfare. I then turned onto State Route 16, a two-lane county road with low-income housing on one side and open fields with bushy trees on the other. It was the kind of neighborhood where people still hung their wash out on clotheslines. There was a large Baptist church and scattered mobile homes. In many respects, everything seemed normal.

Finally, I caught my first glimpse of the prison compound. It was a sprawling, three-story, lime-green giant. It looked like an industrial plant, or textile mill. The guard towers were scattered throughout the complex, which was surrounded by barbed wire fences. I drove past the main gate, located directly across from what looked to be a large cow pasture without any cows. American and Florida state flags hung over a large archway bearing the words "Florida State Prison" in bright orange.

I was driving about five m.p.h. at this point, trying to take in as much on first impression as possible. A group of inmates was playing baseball in a field off to the right side of the main gates. It looked no more organized than a sandlot game, but the players appeared to be enjoying themselves.

Behind them was a group of buildings I later learned to be the P, Q, R, S and T wings, otherwise known as Death Row. At this moment Ray and Susan Cary were probably talking in Q Wing, which contains the holding cells for inmates who are about to be executed. The state's 2,200-volt electric chair is there, too.

After passing the prison, I crossed a tiny wooden bridge that led to what looked like a military base. It was actually a little correctional village. There were some minimum security prisons, a work camp, and, for some odd reason, a meat packing and processing plant. But mostly there were houses and apartments, living quarters for the prison employees and their families.

Yellow ribbons and big American flags were everywhere. The Persian Gulf War buildup was in full swing and people here wanted the rest of the country to know that they supported the troops. The streets were quiet except for an occasional pickup truck zooming by, complete with gun rack.

I found a semi-secluded side street and parked, and wandered for a bit before stumbling upon a yard sale. After a few minutes, it became quite obvious that this was the most exciting thing going on in town. Pickup after pickup stopped by and whole families climbed out to pore over the merchandise, mostly old clothes and paintings on velvet of Elvis or western scenes. I looked at the stuff, too, not because I was interested in buying, but because it was one of the only ways I could think of to start a conversation about the death penalty.

It turned out that I had picked the right house. The owner, a slight, gritty looking fellow in dirty gray overalls with a cigarette hanging from one side of his mouth, was a guard at the state prison. He wasn't only a guard, but also the guy in charge of the generator that feeds the electric chair.

David was uncomfortable answering questions, and asked that I not use his last name. He couldn't understand what a journalist from Southern California was doing in his front yard. He got nervous when I mentioned the impending Ray Clark execution — not because he was apprehensive, but because he was afraid he was going to have to go to work and miss the football game that afternoon. David didn't even know an execution was scheduled, but he said that's not unusual. Executions happen so often in Florida, he said, people hardly pay attention any more.

"I was here when they cranked up the chair in 1979," David muttered in a soft, drawling monotone. "It was big news for a while, then nothing. The more executions there are, the more the excitement dies down. People just don't care.

"Executions always used to be on the front page of the newspaper," he said. "Now execution stories look like classified ads."

We talked about his job, and I asked if he ever felt so much stress or remorse for a condemned man that he wanted to quit. It was a stupid question. To people like David, Death Row isn't a moral issue; working on Death Row puts food on the table. It's that simple.

"If you've got a problem with your job, then you've got to get another job," David said. "There are rights and wrongs in everything. There are faults in every system. Sure, the job is stressful, and it gets to you after a while. I started working in the prison when I was 18, and it was bad then. But it's just part of my living. I pretty much support the death penalty, anyway, and I get paid for it."

David said he knew Ray as well as he knew most of the other Death Row inmates. He has seen many.

"There was one guy, I hated to see him go," David said after pausing to sell a stuffed animal. "There were no tears, but I liked him. He'd call me a sorry son of a bitch and I'd call him a sorry son of a bitch, y'know, just joke around. He was scary, though, a drug addict. He sure was a crazy son of a bitch."

Despite living and working so close to so many supposedly dangerous people, David said he wasn't worried about retaliation or being attacked. He said some of the minimum-security inmates cut people's lawns and are working when the kids come home from school. It's just like living on a military base, he said, and everyone knows the rules.

"People here are trained in firearms," David said. "We all hunt, we all know how to shoot. If an inmate escapes, he won't come here. Look around," he said, pointing toward a truck coming up the road. "The pickup is the average type of vehicle around here. Pretty soon, California will start executing people and become just like Florida. Deep down, we're all just a bunch of rednecks."

Before I could follow up on his unique assessment, David was already off wooing another customer. He was close to making a deal on his old lawnmower, and he didn't want to be disturbed.

His wife and her friend, however, didn't mind talking amid the flea market atmosphere. They were seated behind a large card table stacked with hand-me-down clothing, trinkets, children's toys and assorted other junk. Her kids, all four of them, were running about the yard, occasionally looking toward us and wondering who the stranger was with the note pad, tape recorder and nosy questions.

We started talking about Ted Bundy. David's wife said the entire cow pasture across from the prison was full of people the day of his execution, and cars were parked along the bridge and into her neighborhood.

She didn't feel much remorse for Bundy or regret for the way people rejoiced at his death. "He brought it all on himself," she said. That's when her friend piped up to offer a different opinion.

"Bundy deserved to die, but the celebrations were morbid," she said. "It was a little much."

I started to enjoy this little exchange when business really began to bustle. I wanted to stay, but the only way I could justify hanging around would be to buy something, and I didn't have the money or the inclination for that. I left the two women and David to their business, and I walked back to the car to continue mine.

You might think that life in Starke would be different on the day of a scheduled execution. But as far as I could tell, life couldn't have been more mundane. I saw nothing unusual as I drove past the prison again and headed toward town. Some inmates were exercising in the yard, and a small procession of cars was leaving the prison gates. But there was no highway patrol roadblock, no media, no crowds. Just the hot sun and the yard sale.

It was 2 p.m. now, and the Denny's downtown was nearly empty. This gave me plenty of time to quiz my waitress— an attractive, twenty-something woman who lived in the trailer park behind the motel — about the death penalty. Linda, much to my surprise, opposed capital punishment, an unpopular position in these parts.

"I don't believe in it," Linda said, cautiously looking around to see if anyone was listening. "It doesn't make sense. Maybe if they killed them right away...but that's not how our system works. I'm in the minority here, but that's what I believe.

"They're having one tonight?," she said with surprise after I told her about Ray. "No, I didn't know that. That's terrible."

Linda, too, told me about the Bundy execution. It seems that everyone in Starke has a Bundy story; it's almost folklore, the kind of thing that parents will pass on to their kids. Linda said she even has a scrapbook with all of the newspaper stories about the execution.

"I was in the restaurant the night Bundy was killed," Linda said. "There were reporters everywhere. It was like a big birthday party. The other executions have been no big deal. It was like they never happened."

Linda's gentle, honest voice made my pancakes taste better than they probably should have. People in this part of the country seemed to be less inhibited than people on the West Coast. There are few pretensions and a sense of individuality you have to appreciate. Sometimes, however, that individuality was hard for me to swallow — Linda's boss, for example. She believed capital punishment was as necessary as food, clothing and shelter. And she didn't mince her words.

"I think every scumbag should get the death penalty," she said without batting an eye. "Everyone who murders, attempted murder, rape, whatever. I'm a little prejudiced, I guess. My little sister was murdered in Illinois. They never caught the guy, but if they did I would want him executed, and I would want to do it myself. I would at least want to watch. I mean, my God, she was only 9 years old!

"So there's an execution tonight," she said, having finally calmed down enough to let me pay my check. "It doesn't affect me one way or the other." She said she would be sure to watch for the lights to dim when Ray is executed.

Linda wished me good luck as I left to roam the streets some more. I thanked her for talking to me and, though I didn't dare say anything, I admired her for being able to keep her spirits up while living in what felt to me like such a dark place.

Not unexpectedly, I didn't meet any more Lindas. I talked to dozens of people who all told me the same things: The death penalty is good, it should be done quicker, and why are you asking so many questions?

One of the more colorful responses I got was from Chris Crew, an attendant at the local Exxon station. Crew was going back and forth from helping customers — there weren't many — to watching the University of Florida football game. Interviewing him was like trying to talk to two tennis players in the middle of a match, but I persevered.

Of course, he first had to share his opinion on Ted Bundy. "It took 10 years and $2 million to kill Bundy," Crew said, shaking his head in disbelief. "What they should have done is let him loose in Lake City, where he committed the murders, and he wouldn't have lasted 10 minutes."

Crew was the only person I met who actually knew that Ray Clark was scheduled for execution in less than two hours. He was betting, however, that the execution would be stayed, "just like all his other execution dates."

Crew's main gripe was that there was too much time — and too much money spent — between conviction and execution.

"They either need to just do it or don't," said Crew, now washing a customer's windshield. "They just piss around with all that money, that's what I can't stand. Those people ain't worth that. I rather they just put 'em in a real shitty prison.

"If the death penalty were quick it might be a deterrent. But the way it is now don't serve no purpose. If they could find a way to do it without spending all that money, then it would deter crime." Nevertheless, Crew said capital punishment may not be for everybody.

"It depends on the crime," he said. "Like that guy who decapitated and mutilated them girls in Gainesville. Once they catch him and they know it's him, why take the chance of him getting out and doing it again? If a horse breaks its leg, you shoot it, right?

"It's all politics now," Crew said, finally settling back to watch the rest of the game. "Well, if somebody comes in and says they're going to do away with the death penalty, then they're not going to get elected. At least not in the state of Florida."

It was time for me to get back to my car and over to the prison for the execution. I thanked Crew for his time and walked the four blocks back to my car. It had been a long, taxing day. I was physically and emotionally drained, and not just a little depressed, yet I felt as if the day were only beginning. I still had a lot of work to do.

My thoughts turned to Ray, sitting in his holding cell with Susan Cary by his side. I wondered what he was thinking, whether he held out any hope that he would receive his third stay in less than a week. I wondered if he wanted to die, wanted to get it over with. I wondered what he had chosen for his "last meal".

I don't know what made me turn on the radio. Maybe it was procrastination, not wanting to face the inevitable. Maybe it was hope, or wishful thinking. Whatever the reason, I turned on my car radio before driving toward the prison; it already was tuned to the local National Public Radio affiliate. The time was 5:05 p.m.

"Raymond Clark, sentenced to die at 6:01 tonight for the murder of a Pinellas County businessman, has received an 11th-hour stay of execution from a federal appeals court." I didn't know whether to feel cheated or elated. I simply couldn't believe it.

My mind raced back to Missouri, when I was part of a pack of journalists gathered to cover the execution of Gerald Smith. "It's not gonna happen tonight," the prison spokesman told us. The sense of relief I felt then washed over me now.

It's not gonna happen tonight. It could, according to the news report, happen in the next 48 hours, but I knew it wasn't going to happen tonight.

Few in Starke would notice one way or the other, except perhaps for David, who would be able to stay home and count his yard sale money instead of going to work. After all, executions are to Starke what space shuttle launches are to Cape Canaveral — normal, ordinary, and routine.

I decided to drive by the prison on my way back to Gainesville. This time there were no baseball players, no cars or pickup trucks, just the pale orange Florida sun descending behind the lime-green prison walls. Luckily for Ray, he would be able to see that sun rise another day. But unfortunately for him and the nearly 300 other men of Florida's Death Row, no one around here would give a damn.

According to my copy of the Sunday morning *Gainesville Sun*, Ray's execution was rescheduled for 7:01 Monday morning. Because it was so early, I decided to check out of my hotel and spend the night in Starke. Ray's chances really looked bleak this time. His only recourse now was with the U.S. Supreme Court, a body which rarely grants 11th-hour stays and which already refused to intervene on Ray's behalf the previous week.

The federal circuit court in Atlanta, it turned out, had granted the last stay about the same time I had rolled into Starke the previous morning. But upon further review, the court rejected Ray's appeal. So the Monday morning date looked like a go. This would really be it. Raymond Clark was really going to die.

Which, of course, meant that the chances of me talking to Susan were about the same as former Florida Governor Bob Martinez giving Clark a commutation. She called just to tell me that she wouldn't have time to talk. After spending Saturday with Ray, she was heading back to the prison to stay up with him through the night.

"I'm going to be with him until he goes to the chair," she said, her voice filled with exhaustion and anxiety. "He doesn't have any family here. I don't want him to be alone when he dies."

I didn't sleep much either that night in Starke. I kept waiting for the lights to flicker, or for another miracle that could put this off for another day, or even a few more hours. But I knew that wasn't going to happen. Ray's moment had come. He was going to be killed by the state of Florida, and there wasn't a thing I or Susan or anyone else could do about it.

Ray now knew the exact time, date and place of his death. He knew the procedure. He knew the method. He knew everything except how it would feel the second before he would stop feeling, forever. I could have a heart attack and die tonight, be killed on a bus next year, or die in my sleep at age 95, but Ray didn't have to guess anymore. His death would be by appointment, a pre-arranged ceremony with all the ritual of an ancient sacrifice.

I awoke Monday morning to complete blackness. I hadn't slept long or terribly well, and a quick shower and a cup of coffee didn't help much. It felt more than just a little bit surreal as I got into my car and began the 15-minute drive toward the prison.

I didn't even bother to turn on the radio this time to see if anything had changed. I knew it hadn't. The feeling of death was so thick around here that it seemed the night was doing all it could to keep the sun from coming up.

It was still dark at 6 a.m. when I arrived at the prison. The only lights were those of the prison compound and the other correctional facilities nearby. The air was a chill 50 degrees, much colder than anything I had felt on my trip so far, though this was the latter part of November. A blanket of thin mist hovered above the prison, where four police cars were parked by the front gate. A group of state troopers stood huddled together, trying to keep warm rather than keep guard. They talked quietly, waiting for it all to be over.

Television satellite trucks were setting up shop in the cow pasture across the road. There also were a couple of cops directing traffic into the area, looking as bored as their colleagues.

I parked next to one of the television trucks and walked toward an open area of the field where a small band of death penalty protesters had gathered. About 50 yards away, a man in his 60's was leaning against a gray Chevy sedan and staring at the prison. Actually, he was staring at three white vans parked by the westernmost building. That's where the electric chair was located, on the bottom floor. When an inmate is officially declared dead, someone steps outside the building and waves a white handkerchief to let the public know that the state's business has been completed.

Still trying to keep my sleepy eyelids from slamming shut, I ambled over to where the group of 10 protesters were lighting a bed of white candles and encircling them with white signs which read "Why do we kill people to show that killing people is wrong," and "Only a sick society rejoices in anyone's murder" in black lettering. Each protester — women and men, including a minister — also held a tall, thin candle, cupping their hands to shield the flame from the brisk wind.

One woman, the president of Gainesville Citizens Against the Death Penalty, was about to be interviewed by a television reporter, a bright-eyed fellow who looked as if he just stepped off the pages of *Gentleman's Quarterly*. Since he was the working press and I, according to Florida, was the out-of-work press, I stood aside while he searched for some sound bites.

His first question, as it turned out, was also mine: Why so few protesters?

"I don't think people are ignoring the execution," she said. "It's just the time of day. Most people are on their way to their jobs right now. We speak for those who couldn't come out because of their work schedule. There would have been a lot more people if the execution were held Saturday."

Apparently, that's all the reporter wanted or needed, because he didn't ask anything else. He walked off toward the guy with the Chevy, taking his cameraman and his London Fog trench coat with him.

It was my turn. The woman, Lynn Smith, was bundled in a black overcoat and wearing a red beret. Clutching her candle close to her chest, she told me why Florida is the death-penalty capital of the United States.

"People here aren't educated about the death penalty," she said, protecting her candle as if it were a small child. "There is a lot of poverty and racism here. Those factors also contribute to more people ending up on Death Row.

"Most people on Death Row did not have good representation in the beginning, and there are not many resources to have good appeals," she continued. "Most people under capital punishment don't have capital."

Like the abolitionists I had met before, Lynn was optimistic that a reason for some hope was just around the corner. Sometimes, she said, it's just her and another woman standing in the field, bearing witness to the state's murder. Other times there are 50 people gathered to protest.

That number still seemed low to me.

"Well, that's a lot for here," she said, somewhat embarrassed. "Our mailing list is huge, but people just don't want to come."

As we talked, we were joined by another woman in a jeans jacket and a permed mop of blonde hair. She introduced herself as Mrs. James McCrae. The name pierced me like an arrow. James McCrae was one of the Florida inmates I was scheduled to meet before my clearance was denied. Mrs. McCrae seemed genuinely happy that I had wanted to talk to her husband, and spent about five minutes ranting about the prison officials not granting me access. Fortunately, I didn't need special clearance to talk to her.

She told me her husband had been on Death Row for nearly 18 years, and that they had been married for a year and a half. She said he has been on deathwatch twice, and that while his spirits are high, he's not very hopeful that he'll get his sentence reduced to life in prison.

When I asked her why she married him, she looked at me sort of funny and smiled. "Because I love him," she said. "Why else do you marry people? He's a great guy."

Now it was my turn to be embarrassed. That was, of course, the right answer. I should have remembered that from my conversation back in Washington with November — "I didn't

Members of the Gainesville Citizens Against the Death Penalty protest the execution of Ray Clark, Florida State Prison, Starke

marry a man on Death Row," November had said. "I married Bobby."

Some things that people do aren't for us to understand, or to analyze, or to judge. In many cases, these women who marry condemned men are lonely or have come from abusive or broken homes. If loving someone on Death Row gives them reason to go on living, then so be it. Take away one life, give life to another.

Mrs. McCrae excused herself and rejoined her group, which was about to bow heads in prayer for Ray. Clasping hands, they encircled the bed of candles and asked God to do what Florida Governor Martinez would not: spare Ray's life.

But there was now less than 30 minutes to go before the execution. This would not be a morning for miracles.

No group of people was happier about that than the two men and one woman who were standing together on the other side of the pasture. I had seen one of the men earlier next to the Chevy, and as it turns out, he drove 100 miles from Georgia just to be at Clark's execution.

The sun had finally made its presence known, though its light was dull and the air still carried an icy breeze. While the protesters prayed, Larien Cone, the man with the Chevy, told me why he supported the death penalty, and about his brother, who was killed by someone currently on Florida's Death Row.

"I guarantee you'd think twice before killing somebody if you knew you were going to get the electric chair in six months' time," Cone said, angry that executions like Ray's take so many years. "That's plenty of time. Edward Dean Kennedy shot my brother nearly 10 years ago, and he's still on Death Row. He's had two death warrants, and his case is in Atlanta right now. It's been too long. Ain't no sense in it.

"When he's finally executed, I'll feel that justice will have been carried out. I'll jump for joy when my brother's murderer gets what he deserves."

Cone's eyes never left the building where the electric chair was located. As he spoke, the woman, a wiry, over-tanned type with a blue jean jacket and enormous boots, was ridiculing the nearby protesters.

"They always really turn out," said Sheila Lee in a thick Southern accent. "Bleedin' heart liberals, y'know how it is. The death penalty is right, it's justice, it's the law. A life for a life. They talk about cruel and unusual punishment, well, I think cruel and unusual punishment would be sitting on Death Row thinking up things to file appeals on. Years and years of knowing that you may end up in the electric chair anyway for all your filing. If it were me, I would much rather have it over more quickly."

Lee described herself as a "victim's advocate". She was there, admittedly, just for kicks. Her goal in life, she said, was to be an executioner.

She said she witnessed a Florida execution on July 13, 1984. The inmate was David Lee Washington, otherwise known as Pee Wee, a misleading moniker considering his six-foot frame. Pee Wee, like Ray, was a friend of Joe Ingle's. Joe described Pee-Wee as a reticent man with a troubled soul who deeply regretted his crime — the murder of three people in a Miami ghetto.

Joe didn't witness the execution, but rather joined a circle of about 50 death penalty opponents who had gathered in the cow pasture, much as the small group had done this morning. Joe described the experience in his book, *Last Rights:*

"A Gainesville United Church of Christ minister led the service of song and remembrance of David Washington. Shortly before 7 a.m. we concluded and faced the prison. We remained silent as the minutes passed, approaching the 7 a.m. electrocution. Shortly after 7:15 a.m., the door opened from Q wing and the white handkerchief was waved. It was a signal to the world that the execution was complete. Pee Wee was dead."

Lee had a different perspective on Pee Wee's death. She described the execution for me, an experience which, judging from her excited mood, was something she relished retelling.

"It was fantastic," Lee said with a huge grin. "It's very clinical and unemotional. You're sitting there in rows of chairs and you're separated from the chamber by Plexiglas. You can't see the executioner, he's behind a curtain there.

"That's something I'd like to be," she said, interrupting herself. "I could do that. I really could. I believe in it that strongly." Lee continued her story.

"They lead the prisoner in and sit him down in the chair. Most of them don't struggle, which is a really good thing 'cause there is enough guards to subdue him. If not he could kick the glass out and he'd be right there with us.

"So they seated Washington and put straps around his legs and on the arms," she said, giving a pantomime demonstration. "They put conducting gel on his head, put on the headpiece, and put on a black veil. That was it.

"A prison official was near the phone line to the governor's office and checked to see if there were any last-minute appeals," Lee said. "There weren't any, so he signals the executioner to start the electrocution cycle. It was a two-minute cycle. Washington tensed noticeably, and when the cycle was complete, he slumped. Of course, you couldn't see his face. You could see the sweat through his blue shirt, though, and he was wet. It just took one cycle.

"It didn't affect me emotionally," she said. "I was sitting right in front of him, so he naturally just faced me in the chair. He looked right at me, and all I really felt was thank God, justice has been done. This is the price you must pay for taking a human life." Lee said most of the witnesses handled the experience well, except for one.

"There was this guy from Palm Beach," Lee said, trying to suppress laughter. "He told me he was a police officer, and had been an officer for 10 years. Afterward he said, 'Oh my God, I didn't think it would be like this.' And I thought, jeez! One word flashed across my mind: wimp, wimp, wimp!"

Listening to Lee's story caused me to lose track of time. When I finally glanced down at my watch, it was almost 7:10. The execution was scheduled for 7:01. It had begun. It had been happening the whole time Lee was telling her story.

The protesters still were bowing their heads in prayer. I felt like doing the same, but unfortunately I was stuck on the wrong side of the field. So instead I stared across the road, locking my eyes onto the white vans and Q wing for the final word.

"They're on him now," Cone said, keeping his unblinking eyes trained on the prison.

At 7:10 a man walked out and waved a white handkerchief. Raymond Clark was dead.

Cone clapped quietly, enjoying the moment. Lee, however, had trouble containing her glee. "All right, there's our flag!" she screamed. Turning to me, Lee noticed my subdued composure and prodded, "You haven't been to an execution before, have you?"

I smiled politely, thanked Lee and the others for their time and walked away. The abolitionists continued to pray — and now, to mourn. Instead of joining them I walked to another part of the field where the witnesses and prison officials were being dropped off by one of the white vans.

I cornered Charlotte Sutton, a reporter for the St. Petersburg Times. "He didn't have a last statement; he seemed resigned to the execution," Sutton told me. "He just walked in, sat down, and looked everybody straight in the eye. That was about it. Pretty unremarkable."

Sutton abruptly excused herself and went to join the media pack that had gathered around Bob MacMaster, the Florida prison spokesman with whom I was supposed to meet later that day in Tallahassee, the Florida capital. Because of the delay in the execution, we had rescheduled for Tuesday morning.

MacMaster gave the official description to the gathered press who didn't have an opportunity to witness the proceedings personally. One reporter asked MacMaster to confirm reports that smoke was seen emanating from Ray's leg.

"That happens frequently during an execution," MacMaster said. "About half the time, depending on the composition of the tissue and so forth, when you apply 2,000 volts, the leg electrode occasionally will produce smoke." A nice, clinical explanation —no harm, no foul. Just another day at the office.

I had had enough of Starke. I stood in the field motionless for a while, taking in the scene: reporters scrambling about, some climbing back into their satellite trucks to prepare broadcasts; protesters hugging and crying, consoling each other over the loss of a man none of them knew; death penalty supporters shaking hands, making plans to meet at the next execution.

The show was over. It was time to move on. I drove toward town to grab some breakfast before the three-hour drive to Tallahassee. There was a light mist that in drought-ridden California probably could have passed for rain, but here it just added to the dreariness of a much-too-early morning in north-central Florida.

A couple of miles from the prison, heading toward Starke, I passed kids lined up waiting for the school bus to arrive. Some parents stood with them, while others drove by on their way to work. An elderly man sat on his porch, apparently entertained by the traffic and activity. Chris Crew, bundled in a dark blue jacket, helped a middle-aged woman fill her car's tank with gas.

Life was going on, oblivious to what had just occurred. And that's when it hit me — the handkerchief, Florida's white flag, wasn't a sign of death at all. It was a sign of surrender; it means that there is nothing else to do but to give up. That's what the state of Florida did to Ray. They gave up. They didn't know how to deal with him, so they gave up and killed him.

We do it all the time, really. Human beings aren't very good at taking care of each other. We stink when it comes to communicating our feelings, finding out what bothers us and dealing with whatever problems come our way. We are very good, however, at killing each other. We've been doing it for some time; our species has become quite proficient. Killing is easy — no need to worry about counseling or doing something about poverty. No reason to mess with funding for drug or alcohol abuse programs or for court-appointed lawyers who know something about the law. Just kill.

So the state of Florida — the *people* of Florida — gave up on Ray Clark. They waved the white flag and went about their business. No one would remember anything human about Ray. If they remembered anything, it would be this:

Clark, Raymond Robert. Age 49. Died 11/19/90, at Starke, Florida. The 25th killer executed in the Florida electric chair since 1979. The 142nd killer executed in the United States since 1977, when the death penalty was reinstated by the U.S. Supreme Court. The 222nd killer executed in the Florida electric chair since it first was used in 1924. U.S. Execution #3, 860.

Doctors officially pronounced the killer dead at 7:07 a.m. Eastern Time. The killer's only known relative, his mother, was not with him when he died.

CHAPTER 5

THE DAY AFTER

"The inmate basically feels nothing. You're just there one minute, and the next minute you're gone."
—Bob MacMaster, Florida Department of Corrections public affairs officer

"About 5 percent of the people on our Death Row are innocent."
—Larry Spaulding, Florida's Death Row appeals representative

I pulled into Tallahassee around 2 p.m. Monday, Nov. 19, about seven hours after the execution. I'm not sure if it was because of the execution or that I had gotten up so early, but my stomach wasn't getting along too well with the french toast and eggs I had had for breakfast. But rather than immediately check into a hotel and succumb to a nap or lose myself in Star Trek reruns, I decided to get some exercise and do some exploring.

As capital cities go, this one was hardly majestic. The Capitol building itself looked like a high-rise office, a creamy, white tower with the appearance of a county hospital — very white, very clean, very sterile. The only sense of history to be felt was in a small exhibit area where the Civil War story was retold, and in a mock-up of the old legislative chamber. I was the only one there, and the feeling I got was of being in a shrine.

I was going to walk around Downtown, but I was getting pretty tired and it was starting to get dark. I decided to go back to my motel and watch the local evening news to see how Ray's execution was reported.

Any story, no matter how important, becomes routine after it's been done too many times. The execution was the second story on the 5:30 p.m. news — *after* the sports and weather. One station didn't carry the story at all on its 6 p.m. report.

The first story I saw centered on why there was smoke coming from Ray's leg, and the reaction of the victim's son, Gregory Drake. There was nothing about the protest, nothing about Ray himself. The camera followed Gregory to his car as he prepared to leave.

"I do believe in the fact that every individual is responsible for what you do in your life," Gregory said, "and that if you take someone's life, you should be willing to give for what you've taken." With more images of Gregory walking to his car in the early morning chill, the reporter said, "Gregory Drake has seen the end of his father's killer." Gregory then turns toward the camera and says, "Have a nice day."

The Florida News Network gave a very dry report, resembling the sterile tone of prison bureaucrats:

"The hearse arrived at 6:30 a.m. and the wait began," the reporter said, standing before images of the prison gates and the faithful gathered in the cow pasture. "The signal came at 7:10 a.m. that Clark was dead."

Cut to Bob MacMaster: "He had his last meal at 4:30 a.m., and then he was prepped for execution." I was in the camera shot, standing next to him, taking notes. My head was down so no one could see my face.

"He was led into the execution chamber just before 7 a.m.," MacMaster continued. "The current was applied at approximately 7:01, and pronouncement of death was approximately 7:07."

Cut to Gregory: "The biggest thing unresolved is he never did speak," he said of Ray. "He never gave his side of the story whatsoever. He never expressed any remorse."

THE DAY AFTER

As the hearse left the prison grounds, the reporter continued his commentary: "Clark's body was taken to Gainesville for an autopsy," he said. "His only listed next of kin was his mother, who lives in Connecticut."

End of story. Ray Clark's life was now a footnote in Florida's long history of death — from the Civil War to capital punishment. But unlike the Civil War, there won't be any memorials to Ray Clark or to any other Death Row inmate. It's hard in the South to forget about the Civil War. And it's easy to forget about Death Row.

To be honest, I didn't feel like sticking around Florida much longer. It was just a few days before Thanksgiving, and I was ready for a break. Nevertheless, I didn't want to miss my appointment with MacMaster the next morning. I was interested to hear his side of the execution, and to hear his justifications for the death penalty. There was also still a chance that I would be able to talk to Susan Cary. I was supposed to call her after my meeting with MacMaster, and possibly drive back to Gainesville for an interview. Logistically, it wasn't too pleasing, but I had a hunch it would be worth it.

If there's one thing I learned to count on over the last weekend, it was not to count on Susan being available. That's why I lined up a substitute interview, a lawyer named Larry Spaulding who knew Susan well — in fact, she referred me to him. Larry had the dubious honor of being in charge of Florida's Capital Collateral office, the way station for all of the state's Death Row appeals.

That's how my last full day in Florida seemed to be shaping up. Tonight, however, it was a Motel 6 with cardboard bed sheets and a rotary dial telephone. It didn't matter, though. I couldn't sleep and I didn't have anyone to call. I just sat up, listened to the party next door, and thought about my horrible morning in a cold cow pasture in Starke.

The party was just dying down when I woke up at 7 a.m. I figured I probably fell asleep around 3 or 4 a.m., or whenever it was that the room stopped shaking. I guess I shouldn't have expected too much peace and quiet for $19.95 a night.

Nothing could put me in a bad mood today, however. It was almost Thanksgiving, and I was getting an early start by being thankful that I would be leaving Florida soon.

I got directions to MacMaster's office from his secretary, but it didn't matter — I got lost anyway. MacMaster worked in the large, cement-colored headquarters of the Florida Department of Corrections. The complex was spacious, the employees pleasant. Three different people asked me if I wanted coffee, and that's before I even said who I was.

I was on time, but MacMaster was running late and had not yet arrived. I waited in his office while one of the secretaries made some tea — I had to be difficult — and had a good 10 minutes to review his police credentials, his NRA membership certificate and pictures of his family.

MacMaster came in bursting with apologies. There was a traffic accident near his house, and he had gotten caught in the ensuing bottleneck. He towered over me, and though I'm relatively short, he probably could look down on Wilt Chamberlain. He wore a nicely tailored suit and black boots, with a matching glove on his right hand.

It was his left hand, however, that was mechanical. I was amazed at the ease with which he used it to move some newspapers and arrange some things on his desk. I wanted to ask him about it, but, as I am with most people who have some sort of handicap, I was too embarrassed. Besides, his hand wasn't what I came to talk about.

I got right to the point: What happened to Ray Clark?

"There were a couple wisps of smoke in the area of the leg attachment, but that's normal when you're running over 2,000 volts," MacMaster said, leaning back in his big, black leather chair. "There's nothing he feels, though. He's knocked unconscious right away. It's instantaneous.

"Compared to lethal injection, the electric chair is much, much quicker. And therefore, probably more humane. There's really very little movement. If you apply an electrical current, it will make your muscles tense up, and appear to throw your muscles into contractions. But the inmate basically feels nothing. You're just there one minute and the next minute you're gone."

MacMaster said there was only one time that he actually saw flames during an execution, but that too, he said, was much ado about nothing.

"During the Jesse Tafero execution...there was a problem with the sponge on that one," he said. "There's a sponge placed between the headpiece and the top of the head, and it produced smoke and flames out the sides. It startled everyone that was there, but he wasn't on fire, the sponge was."

MacMaster did his best to play it down, but even avid death penalty proponents agree that the Tafero execution was one of the most brutal and macabre in U.S. history.

Tafero was executed on May 4, 1990, for the killing of four people, including three law enforcement officers. According to media witnesses, Tafero's body reeled backward as flames shot out from the side of his execution mask. His heart was still beating at the end of the cycle, so they hit him again — and there were more flames, and more smoke. Still, his heart kept beating, his chest kept heaving.

So they hit him a third time. There were more flames and smoke, but this time, the heartbeat and breathing stopped. Tafero, finally, was dead.

After the execution, MacMaster told reporters: "The execution was carried out. That's what is the important priority. We'll just try to get the right equipment next time."

MacMaster told me his main job is to talk to the press and prepare media witnesses for executions. Being a witness himself isn't necessarily part of the bargain. Nevertheless, he usually is there, mostly to be in a better position to provide an official account of what occurred. The first execution he attended was that of Beauford White, in August 1987.

"I wondered what my reaction was going to be," MacMaster said, having taken a moment to collect his thoughts. "But when

I saw how clinical, how straight out with precision...there was very little gore. The only thing that was shocking perhaps was realizing that I was going to see somebody killed.

"People don't normally see death," he said. "It's not something you look forward to with glee or anything like that. It's strictly a professional duty in that sense, and I had very little reaction. It was just my job."

The duty has grown even easier over time.

"Now I know what to expect," MacMaster said. "I know how it's going to be done, and it's not something that you have a significant reaction to. You have respect for it, though," he added, perhaps not wanting to sound harsh or cold. "You respect that a group of men are carrying out the most severe punishment that is administered by law. It's not something to be taken lightly. After all, you are seeing a death."

That experience, MacMaster said, did allow him to reflect on his own mortality. We all, he said, need to be aware of the fact that death is not an option, but a certainty.

"Everyone's days are numbered, and we should all be a little more concerned about making good use of those days while we're here," he said. "I don't think the American public as a society is cognizant of the fact that lives are set out for a number of days, and that there is an end for everybody. When you see a death you become more conscious of that. Maybe society would be better, perhaps wiser, if they understood that. But I don't think they have to see executions to do that."

Florida has more than 300 people on its Death Row, making it one of the largest in the country. MacMaster said there is at least one active death warrant — the court order certifying an execution date — ten months out of every year, and that most inmates are executed by their second or third warrant. No one, he said, has ever been executed on the first warrant. From the time of sentencing to the time of execution, MacMaster said the average stay on Death Row in Florida is nine years.

MacMaster admitted that, except for the notorious Ted Bundy, executions don't grab the headlines they used to. From

Florida's first to its most recent, the routine involved in each execution has remained basically the same.

Using Ray's execution as an example, MacMaster said the inmate is moved to a special cell a week before the execution. That cell is about 30 feet from the electric chair, and is constantly watched by a guard to make sure the inmate doesn't try to injure himself, someone else, or somehow escape.

The inmate is allowed to hold media interviews the day before the execution. This was a privilege exploited heavily by Bundy, whose famous television confessions have become a part of Americana.

That evening, the inmate can receive visits. MacMaster said Ray had several visitors, including Susan and some other attorneys. Those visits generally run from 8 p.m. to 1 a.m., and after that the inmate can request that a minister stay with him until 5 a.m. A minister did stay with Ray, MacMaster said. He stayed through Ray's 4:30 a.m. last meal, which consisted of filet mignon, French fries, cobb salad, strawberry shortcake, and chocolate milk. MacMaster said that Ray ate about half of his meal — most of the steak, a few French fries. Then he was taken out of his cell to get his head and lower right leg shaved. That's so the conducting gel and the electrodes would have a clear connection.

Ray showered and put on blue trousers and a white dress shirt. He was led into the execution chamber just a few minutes before the 7 a.m. deadline. After he was strapped in and an electrode was attached to his shaved leg, Ray was asked if he had any final statement. He said no. That ritual completed, the head piece — a metal cap with a leather cover — was placed on his head.

The next procedure is for the superintendent to call the governor and ask if there are any last-minute stays. The superintendent then walks over to the executioner, who is standing behind a partitioned wall out of sight from the witnesses, and nods his head.

That's it. The executioner begins the cycle.

MacMaster said that once the switch is turned, everything is automated. There are three "peaks" in each two-minute cycle, with each peak being a little more than 2,000 volts. It usually doesn't take more than one cycle to kill someone. MacMaster said Ray's electrocution took just about a minute, though it was a few minutes more before doctors officially pronounced him dead.

MacMaster said it's rare when the murder victim's families are allowed to see their relative's murderer killed. The department made an exception for Gregory Drake.

"We usually exclude family members because there is the possibility of an emotional reaction," MacMaster said. "But he had a very measured attitude toward it.

"Obviously, there are a lot of people on Death Row in the South," said MacMaster, gearing for a speech. "This reflects justice as it was chosen by the people. We have one of the most fair justice systems in the world, and I think the numbers on Death Row reflect the will of the people. The punishment is appropriate in relation to the crime."

I told MacMaster about my conversations with townspeople in Starke, and how they generally either supported the death penalty or were indifferent to it. I also mentioned my talk with the prison guard who was in charge of the electric chair, and how he tried to distance himself from the inmates.

That seemed to strike a nerve with MacMaster. First of all, he admonished me not to call them guards, but rather corrections officers. Then the former cop told me how the job requires doing things in an orderly fashion, focusing your energy on professionalism, not emotion.

"Our people are instructed not to become emotionally attached," MacMaster said. "These people aren't on Death Row for jaywalking. It's not unheard of for inmates to devise escape plots that involve even the littlest things. You basically don't trust someone who is in jail for a murder," MacMaster said. "If you do, you're a fool. Once they've killed someone in an illegal manner, they're capable of doing it again."

MacMaster said the officers try to help them somewhat with dealing with the future, though the real life and death stuff is left to the clergy.

"But they're careful not to allow that care and concern to blend into emotional involvement."

This separation of humanity and emotion left me a little puzzled, but I didn't query further, as it was time to go. MacMaster gave me a pile of literature on the Florida corrections system, and we shook hands. He was a nice guy, and I appreciated him offering some of his feelings rather than merely the party line.

It was 10 a.m., time to check in with Susan on the off-chance that we might be able to see each other before I left the state for good. The good news is that when I called her, I got her real voice rather than the one on the answering machine. The bad news is that she was exhausted, and had to be back at the prison that afternoon. I was a little peeved at this point. I really wanted to talk to her in person, and I felt that she wasn't making as much time as she could have. But I was in no position to argue or assume. We simply decided to get together by phone sometime soon, and said good-bye.

It was a good thing I set up that tentative meeting with Larry Spaulding at the Capital Collateral office; I called him after I got off the phone with Susan and confirmed our appointment. With several hours to go until that interview, I picked up every newspaper I could find and went to breakfast. I wanted to see how my colleagues in the print media handled Ray's execution.

The first paper I read was the *St. Petersburg Times*. They played the story on page one, though only because Ray's victim, David Drake, was from the St. Petersburg area. The story, written by the reporter I talked to after the execution, centered on Gregory Drake and his pilgrimage to Starke to see his father's killer executed.

According to the story, Gregory had vowed to see Ray die, and was glad that prison officials lifted their restriction on family members in the witness room. He also said that while he understood the feelings of the death penalty opponents, he didn't agree with them.

"I was raised with 'an eye for an eye, a tooth for a tooth', and with the idea that you're responsible for what you do," Gregory said in the story. "Being raised that way, that's still how I feel."

The story also quoted Gregory's mother, Donna. "I'm happy Clark died gentle," she said. "He didn't fight it."

The article called 49-year-old David Drake's murder "one of the most bizarre crimes St. Petersburg has seen." David, according to the story, was kidnapped by Ray and his homosexual lover, 16-year-old Ty Jeffrey Johnson, in a bank parking lot on April 27, 1977, and was driven away in his new Cadillac.

David wrote his captors a $5,000 check, but they shot him anyway. When they couldn't cash the check, they called Gregory and asked for $10,000 in exchange for his father's life — though he was already dead. Police traced the phone calls and caught the suspects, who led authorities to David's decomposed body on the shore of Tampa Bay.

Ray was on parole for killing a 14-year-old California boy when he was charged with David's murder. Johnson testified against Ray and received 25 years in prison for second-degree murder. He was released in nine.

Susan was quoted describing Ray's mood before the execution.

"He was very courageous, very calm and very concerned about his family and the friends that have stuck by him," she said. "But when we spoke last night, his real concern was for the Drake family. He was really hoping that they can get on with their lives and begin healing and letting go of the anger and pain."

Donna Drake planned to do just that. "I want to live," she said. "I'm going to have a great life."

The Gainesville paper played the story on the front of its second section. The story was actually more in depth than the St. Petersburg piece, going into the execution procedure in great detail, and even quoting some of the death penalty opponents. It also related some of Gregory Drake's frustration.

"Basically, it's over," he said. "It's not going to bring back my father."

The story said Ray "appeared calm" when he was seated in the chair, and that "his eyes were wide as he scanned the witnesses in front of him." During the electrocution, Ray's chest and arms tensed against the leather straps, and then relaxed as the wisps of white smoke rose from his leg.

The worst-coverage award went to the largest paper in the state, perhaps the region. *The Miami Herald* buried the story inside its front section, and used wire copy rather than send their own reporter. It was a cold recitation of the facts — another day, another execution.

I took another walk around the Capitol and adjacent shopping area, and then headed to my meeting with Larry Spaulding. His office, unlike MacMaster's, is in a one-story building that looks more like a converted warehouse than a law office. The state runs both the Department of Corrections and the Capital Collateral Center, but it's obvious that the latter gets the light end of the budget.

Larry's operation handles nearly all Death Row appeals at one point or another. It was established by the state as sort of a public defender's office for capital punishment cases, though the state's conservative lawmakers have done their best to strip much of that funding away. This is the environment Larry works in every day, never knowing when his staff will be cut further, or how much he can spend on any given investigation.

Larry welcomed me into his office, and we talked for several hours between phone calls and harried lawyers rushing in to get a signature or advice. Through it all, Larry was the picture of calm, resting his hands on his belly or stroking his gray beard. He had a country-boy face which went well with his cowboy boots, but spoke like someone who has seen much of the city and the horrors of urban life.

I thanked him for filling in for Susan. Larry was a big fan of hers, and said he admired the way she deals with inmates. Being a lawyer, he said, is the least part of her job.

"She prepares inmates for death," Spaulding said. "She tries to turn it into a positive. Part of it is spiritual, and part of it is...well, if you're dying, it can't be worse than where you are now."

Larry said Susan's caring hand helped him through the first time he attended an execution. He has witnessed eight executions in all. When he arrived at the prison the night before that first time, Larry said he kept telling himself not to like the inmate, not to get attached. But it didn't work. He did care. On top of that, he was scared.

"I was rather nervous, but Susan was so strong," he said. "She already had worked with the inmate and his family, and they knew the odds were against them. The inmate was the one who was to be strapped into the chair, and he was asking if I was all right. I've dealt with my own fear since then, and I'm no longer afraid to talk about death."

Larry added, however, that no amount of counseling from Susan could have prepared him for witnessing that first execution.

"It was just very sick, very barbaric," Larry said. "It was like a military process, very planned. The prison officials were just these people doing their jobs, no more and no less. They might go have a cigarette and play cards, and the execution may not even be a topic of discussion. It was a non-event. That's just really tragic. I guess in order to deal with it, they have to think that the inmates are less than they are."

Larry said Florida puts about one person on Death Row each week. Florida, he said, loves its death penalty.

"Maybe it's a frontier mentality," Spaulding said. "I don't know. Florida is an incredibly diverse state. You have Pensacola, which is really part of south Alabama. Miami is more like New York City, and the west coast is full of people from the Midwest.

"I think it's just that former Governor Bob Graham set the standard," he said. "In order to counter his moderate to liberal image, he became one of the nation's most aggressive governors in regard to supporting the death penalty. Politically, it worked, and Gov. Bob Martinez was elected later because he took a harder line on the death penalty than his Democratic opponent."

Florida, Larry said, doesn't require a unanimous jury verdict to send someone to Death Row. And if a jury votes for life, the judge can change the verdict to death.

"Judges have done that about 130 times," he said. "The public loves it. They think that's tough. Our statute is a prosecutor's dream."

He said the press also helped to fuel the public's demand for capital punishment. Early on, all executions were heavily covered. That has dropped off, of course, except in the case of some notables like Ted Bundy.

Larry said Bundy was the devil incarnate to most Florida residents, and most of the country, for that matter. He violated our innocence, and brought to bear a terrifying reality.

"He was one of us; that scared people," said Larry, who handled some of Bundy's appeals. "He was an articulate, educated, middle-class white man. He was the president of the Young Republicans. And he jerked the system.

"He was worse than a black man because he betrayed us," Larry said. "We could expect it from a black man, but not from him. He destroyed the innocence of Tallahassee. This isn't a place like Miami or New York City, where people get killed. But after Bundy went to the second floor of a sorority house, and murdered in the shadow of the Capitol of the state...there are people here who are vehemently anti-death penalty, and it impacted them."

Nevertheless, he said Bundy didn't deserve to die.

"I don't think anybody deserves to die," he said. "Even Ted Bundy. He probably received the most unfair trial a guilty person ever got. We have people on Death Row who have killed more than Bundy. But Bundy jerked the system. Right until the end."

Larry talked for a while about the overwhelming burden death penalty cases put on the criminal justice system. He said part of the reason for the push to limit appeals is the court's own self-preservation. Many cases are on the average of more than two years behind the initial direct appeal. He said Florida signs about 40 death warrants each year. The cycle never ends.

"If you took a secret ballot of the judiciary, certainly the appellate judiciary, the death penalty would be abolished overnight," Larry said. "Not that most judges aren't in principle pro-death penalty, but we pay too high a price for it.

"The truth of the matter is that for a variety of reasons, a death case at all levels is just incredibly expensive," he said. "We spend much more money on a death case than we do on a non-capital murder. The defense and prosecution put more time into the investigation, and hire better experts.

"If the death penalty is ever abolished, it's not going to be on principles, it's going to be on dollars. That's a rather cynical way to look at it, but if the public realizes they can't afford it, then they'll abolish it."

The public, or at least the state Legislature, already tried to abolish Larry's job. It was a U.S. Supreme Court case brought by Joe Giarratano against the state of Virginia that saved the office. The case established a right to counsel in post-conviction death cases, and prompted the Florida lawmakers to back off.

Larry said he doesn't necessarily oppose the death penalty from a strictly moral standpoint. Rather, he has seen how it works, and doesn't think it ever could be made fair.

"The crimes that you deal with are all horrible crimes," he said. "That's a given. What we're concerned with is whether the person received a fair trial, and whether the person actually is guilty. There are several cases where we are absolutely convinced that they're not. Statistically, I'd say about 5 percent of the people on our Death Row are innocent.

"On paper, we have one of the best, if not the best, clemency systems in the country," he said. "But the governor never pays attention to it. Granting clemency would have negative political fallout. But it is never politically disadvantageous to sign a death warrant."

It was beginning to get dark, and I had another long drive ahead. We had talked much longer than either of us had planned, and I thanked him for the opportunity. Susan or no Susan, my day certainly wasn't a loss.

<h1 style="text-align:center">THE DAY AFTER</h1>

I decided to stop in Pensacola for the night, which is right on the Alabama border. I had to be in Alabama the next day, but judging from my maps, it didn't seem like southern Alabama had much to offer in the way of motels.

My trip to Alabama was part design, part coincidence. First and foremost, I happened to be in the neighborhood. I also had established some contacts through one of my former colleagues from the newspaper back home. He once worked in Alabama — and practically every other state — and gave me the names of some key people from Alabama's death penalty past and present.

Charlie Jones was the warden at Holman Prison in Atmore, home of Death Row. He supposedly was a no-nonsense type of warden, who surprised people by offering his condemned prisoners the opportunity to earn college degrees.

I was more interested, however, in J.D. White. He used to be the warden at Holman, and was there in 1983 when Alabama used its electric chair for the first time since reinstatement. That may not seem like a big deal, but the execution was botched, forcing several cycles of current and very visible agony before James Evans was pronounced dead. For whatever reason, White left the prison soon after to take over a minimum security institution in the northern part of the state.

Last but not least, there was my favorite, mostly because of his name: District Attorney Jimmy Fry. It may sound funny, but Fry apparently has never lost a death case, which is nothing to laugh at.

Because of Thanksgiving, I decided to split my Alabama excursion into two trips. Tomorrow I would go to see Jones in Atmore, and that afternoon head north to Atlanta for the holiday weekend. My adventuresome spirit was strong, but it didn't include spending four days in Alabama over a holiday. I had been to Atlanta before and loved it, and I had some interviews there as well. Some of the biggest death penalty cases — the one that abolished capital punishment in 1972 and the one that reinstated it in 1976 — came out of Georgia, so it was a state I felt I couldn't miss.

Before getting back on the highway, I decided to drive past the Capitol one last time. I'm not sure why, really. Maybe I wanted to give it another chance to impress me.

While the Capitol again failed to make an impression, what I saw across the street at the Supreme Court building did. Parked on the sidewalk in front of the domed courthouse was a white prison van, just like the one that was outside the execution chamber when Ray was killed. It was just parked there, as if waiting for the court to toss out its next sacrifice.

I stared at the courthouse and the van, and then drove toward the highway. I popped my Billy Bragg cassette into the tape player, and re-wound it to the lyric that would forever remind me of Florida, Ray Clark, and Death Row:

"This isn't a court of justice, son. This is a court of law."

CHAPTER 6

YELLOW MAMA

"We live for life, we don't live for death. A person is going to live as long as he can."
— Charlie Jones, warden of Holman State Prison, Alabama.

"The length of the cycle depends on if you have any malfunctions or not, the inmate's weight, and how much salt he's consumed. A lot of people don't realize that salt affects the amount of current that will go through your body."
— Assistant warden, Holman State Prison.

I woke up in Pensacola without a clue as to how long it would take me to get to Atmore and the Holman Prison. It didn't look far on the map, but maps rarely take such things into account as two-lane roads infested with pick-up trucks. With that encouraging thought in mind, I checked out of the Red Roof Inn and continued west. It wasn't long before I was across the state line and out of Florida for good. Psychologically, however, I had already left the day before.

I tried as best I could to put the past few days behind me and concentrate on what lay ahead. Everything was going to move fast now, as I had a certain number of interviews and a very tight window in which to do them. I had to stop thinking about Florida, or it would cloud my ability to do a decent job.

As I expected, I rolled into town early. I usually hate doing that, since there is only so much time you can kill by reading the local newspaper. But in this case I was glad, because after driving around for about 20 minutes, I realized that I had absolutely no idea where the prison was.

Atmore seemed as if it were stuck in a time warp. It was a small town with few main streets and plenty of old American cars. Either the prison was disguised as a pharmacy, or it was somewhere on the outskirts of town, which could be anywhere. There were outskirts all over the place.

I guess I had been spoiled by previous states where directions to prison facilities are plainly marked — not so in Alabama. Of course the prison isn't going to be smack dab in the middle of the town square, but you would think there would be an arrow to assist wayward travelers and incompetents like myself.

Fortunately, just as I was about to give up and do something intelligent like call the prison for directions, I spotted a white van that looked like it belonged to the state. I'm not sure how I came to that conclusion, other than it reminded me of the Florida van. Nevertheless, I threw caution out the window and decided to follow it.

The only marking visible from the two-lane highway was a brown, wooden sign which read "Department of Corrections, Holman Unit." Next to that was a small guard hut which looked like it hadn't been used in years. I turned right at the sign onto another two-lane road, this one made of dirt. There were absolutely no signs of life in any direction.

Eventually, the road ended and I was at Holman, an old, red brick structure with an emphasis on practicality rather than aesthetics. It was small compared to the sprawling Florida complex. Then again, Florida has more than 300 Death Row inmates while Alabama has about 110, and only 85 of those are at Holman.

I parked my car in the dirt lot, gathered my things and started walking toward two large metal gates. Before I reached the first one, however, a female voice boomed down at me from the guard tower above.

"What are you doing?" the voice said.

I told her I was a reporter with an appointment to see Warden Charlie Jones. She looked at me for a second, and then gave me permission to go ahead. I pushed through the gates and walked into the administration building, which is adjacent but not attached to the prison itself. After all my directional problems, I actually was on time, and the secretary said I could walk right into Jones' office.

My first glimpse of Charlie Jones almost made me burst out laughing. He looked like every warden in every movie ever made — a living, breathing stereotype of Southern justice. He weighed about 250 pounds with a beer belly, double chin and no apparent neck. He wore boots that were covered with mud, a large black hat and a white, open-collar shirt.

He looked at me for a good five seconds before saying hello. He rocked in his big leather chair and stared out the window, and said in a deep Southern drawl that he had "forgot" about our appointment, and wanted to know how long it would take. Not a great way to start, but I persevered.

A more than 20-year veteran of the department, Jones was an officer at Holman before becoming its warden. He had to oversee an execution almost immediately, in the summer of 1988. He was a busy man that summer. He had to coordinate the security, make sure all the equipment worked, and see to it that the inmates got what they needed, too.

"It's an experience you can't describe," Jones said. "It's a hell of a time, stressful and scary. You want to do it right. You've got to do it, and you want to do it in the most humane way possible. The least little annoyance in the routine can throw the whole thing out of kilter.

"I'm totally responsible for it, and yeah, it affects you," he said. "That's not to say it's not right, that the guy don't deserve it, or that the death penalty ain't right. That's not for me to say; it's just for us to do, by law. I don't feel guilty about it. I don't carry the load for what the inmate did."

Jones refused to give his personal opinion on the death penalty. That was okay; it just enticed me to probe further. Since he wouldn't tell me his views, I asked why he thought the public supported capital punishment so strongly.

"They're tired of the stuff that's going on," Jones said in his best Alabama drawl, "and they believe capital punishment is the only way to deal with it. It would be kind of hard to go right around here and find someone who would say do away with it. People here support the death penalty now and they supported it 21 years ago. Alabama hasn't changed."

I knew what answer to expect from my next question, or at least I thought I did. I was going to ask how he felt toward the inmates, and was sure Jones was going to say something to the effect of: "What a bunch of lousy sons-of-bitches."

I was wrong. Very wrong.

"These are the best group of guys I've ever had," Jones said. "There's just no problems on Death Row right now. We've made some changes there, positive changes. I think they are changes in their favor."

It would be hard to argue with that. Jones' inmates are allowed to have television sets, a radio and a cassette tape player. They can make phone calls as often as they want — so they can be in better touch with their attorneys — and have extensive visiting privileges. They also can go to college. They can take one class per quarter, and eventually earn enough credits for an associate degree.

This is hardly a prison run by an iron fist. Somewhere behind the stereotypic warden, there is a heart. But Jones refuses to believe, as some in the state have claimed, that he is coddling the condemned.

"When you take a person away from all of the people he knows by confining him in a five-by-eight foot cell — and I don't give a damn what you give him — you've done some damage," Jones said defensively. "He's allowed out of that cell 45 minutes a day. He can shower every other day. He eats prison food, which is not bad but it's also not what mother used to make, and he's far from any Holiday Inn or a life of luxury.

"If you talk to a relative of a murder victim, then they might think that things are too cushy," Jones said. "But if you talk to a regular person, they don't care nothin' about it. Since we've made some changes, we've had no problems."

I was satisfied with his answer, but there was no stopping Jones now. He was on a roll.

"How do you punish a guy who's in a one-man cell all day?" Jones said, pushing his point. "A person living in general population gets to move and walk around, and if he gets mouthy to an officer they lock him up. The cell they put him in for punishment is just like the one that the guy on Death Row lives in all the time.

"So how do you punish him? You've got to give a Death Row inmate something extra, so you can have something to take away from him if he gets out of line.

"The way I like to manage is I'll treat these people the way they want to be treated, as long as they'll let me," Jones said. "If you want to hurt a Death Row person right now, I mean really cut him to the bone, then go ahead and take the television out of his cell. It's just hell on Earth for him when you do that. That's why we have so few problems."

Jones was most defensive about his college education program. "What you have to understand is that's a community down there," he said. "It's a town with 85 residents. If we can get them doing something that's constructive, positive, then they are going to take better care of their surroundings and themselves, and they will stop hassling the officers. What we save is far beyond what we spend on any class.

"I took a lot of heat when the program started," he said, "but their health while they're living down there is what I have to look at."

Jones leaned back, exhausted from his lengthy explanation. He began to look fidgety again, as if he knew what I was thinking and wanted to leave before I could articulate it. Here he was, this big ol' redneck from a Southern prison telling me he's concerned about a condemned man's health. It just didn't seem to fit, and though I didn't use those exact words, I told him I was confused.

Jones stared out the window and thought. He then swung his chair around and looked me square in the eye.

"We live for life, we don't live for death," Jones said, as if the answer to the question was plainly obvious. "Me and you do that, and it's the same way for them. A person is going to live as long as he can."

With that, Jones asked if I wanted to see the prison and the room where they keep the electric chair. How could I refuse? I had never seen an electric chair up close before, much less one with a nickname.

That's right, a nickname. It wasn't one the prison officials used, at least not in public, but according to my reporter friend, everyone refers to Alabama's electric chair as Yellow Mama. Why? Because it's painted yellow. The "Mama" part I haven't figured out yet.

Jones and I shook hands, and as I walked out of his office, I watched him nestle back into his chair and stare out toward the Alabama sky. It was mid-afternoon, and the sun hovered gently over the trees near the prison's main guard tower. It seemed Jones really liked that window, as if he drew strength from it. In any case, he was a man willing and able to see beyond the darkness of prison life.

Although he wouldn't say whether he supported the death penalty, I got the sense that Jones wouldn't be too broken up if capital punishment were repealed. The death penalty is something he's forced to deal with, and if there were no executions, he would be just as happy, probably happier.

I don't think he likes doing what he has to do, preparing inmates for life just so they can be killed. I don't he think he likes that at all.

My tour guide was an assistant warden, a thin, preppy-looking fellow in a crisp, white shirt and tasteful striped tie. We did the small talk, but I wasn't really paying attention, and I don't think he was, either. I still had Charlie Jones on the brain, and besides, the noisy prison corridor didn't leave much room for concentration.

Inmates in white t-shirts were running around doing kitchen duty, preparing for that evening's spaghetti dinner, while others slouched against the walls listening to Walkman cassette players. But every eye was on us, no doubt about it. I couldn't blame them, since I was toting a camera and other journalistic junk, but it was somewhat unnerving.

I felt better once we got to the end of the hall, walked through a barred doorway and turned a corner. The noise fell away, and as we made another quick turn to the left, it was silent. We stood at the end of a long hallway. A basketball lay at the other end, and there was nothing else except a lone cell and two large, blue doors.

The cell, I was told, was for problem inmates who officials fear may be suicidal. There was a young man in the cell when we walked past who couldn't have been more than 18. He watched us go by as if we were the only people in the world.

We stopped in front of the second door, and my guide pulled out a set of keys. He opened the door and led me into a room that wasn't any larger than the bedroom I had while growing up. In the center was Yellow Mama, a wooden giant with leather straps draped over its arms and legs. There was an electrode on the floor, and another one on the seat.

The electrode connectors were on the left side of the wall behind the chair, which I learned was built by an English cabinet maker. They transported the current from the power supply room next door. On the right side were two white lights, from which hung a yellow sign with "ready" emblazoned in black letters. I was told that the sign was shown to the executioner in the power room when the procedure was to set to begin.

In front of the chair was the witness room — we didn't have the key for that — with two rows of seats and a black phone to the governor's office.

It took a few minutes before I realized I was face to face with a killing machine. There it was, silent and eerily inviting, as if it were made of smooth leather rather than painted wood. I snapped

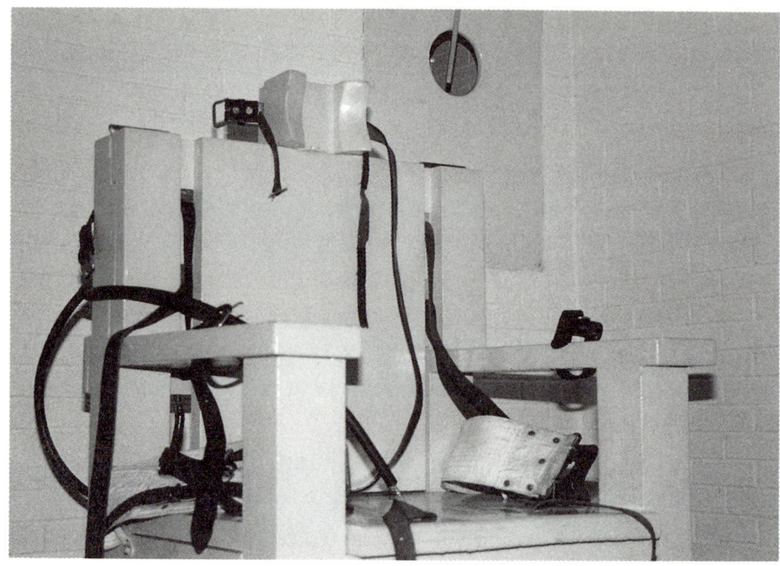

"Yellow Mama," Alabama's electric chair, Holman State Prison, Atmore

photos of it in the same way I would attempt to record the presence of an ancient artifact or some other earthly wonder.

The power supply room — or executioner's chamber — looked like something out of a World War II Army surplus store. The generator hardly seemed able to generate enough power to run a blow dryer, much less produce 2,000 volts of life-ending electricity. But I was assured it worked. My guide said there was a back-up generator in case anything went wrong.

"Only one of a team of three people actually pulls the switch," the warden said. "The length of the cycle depends on if you have any malfunctions or not, the inmate's weight, and how much salt he's consumed. A lot of people don't realize that salt affects the amount of current that will go through your body."

We dawdled for a while and then went back down the hallway to a little rest area with soda machines and benches. Some inmates were outside playing basketball, and there was a stairway nearby leading up to Death Row. The Row was located directly above Yellow Mama.

The warden went to get a drink, so I sat down at one of the benches where a guard was taking a break. We talked a bit about basketball, one of my favorite subjects, though eventually we couldn't escape the topic he dealt with every day.

The warden stood nearby as 35-year-old Melvin Ramsey and I talked, so I'm not sure if Ramsey's comments were truly spontaneous. He was gracious nonetheless.

Ramsey said things have calmed down at the prison since John Evans was killed in 1984. Everybody, he said, does their best to get along.

"As the number of deaths...as the number of executions increased, both sides have become accustomed to it, and tensions don't get as high," Ramsey said. "It's just not as disruptive now."

Ramsey said controlling your emotions, and putting them in proper perspective, is a big part of the job. You have to learn, he said, not to miss anybody.

"It's emotional because you're dealing with human beings," he said. "But as soon as someone's cell is vacated, he's replaced by another inmate who needs us to take care of him. So we don't have time to sit around and say we miss a particular inmate.

"The longer you're here, the more you're able to accept that you're here to do a job. They're human beings and we treat them as such, but I'm able to work here and keep things in perspective. We are not the reason they're here, and we spend very little time on a personal basis with them. You have to subconsciously keep in mind who you're working around."

The assistant warden walked up as soon as Ramsey finished his sentence and told me it was time to go. In fact it was getting late, and I still had several hours of driving to do before I could expect to be in Atlanta for Thanksgiving Eve. I didn't have anything planned the next day, except sleeping and scrounging up a gourmet feast from my cooler. Tuna fish sandwiches and chips are not traditional Thanksgiving fare, but it was either that or

Denny's, and frankly, a fast-food, solo holiday feast was an even more demoralizing thought.

As we walked back to the administration area, we were stopped by one of the inmates who complained to the warden about not getting his mail on time. The warden smiled and consoled the inmate, promising to take care of the situation immediately.

That's what he told the inmate, anyway. He told me, "They're always complaining about something. Like we have any control over the goddamn mail."

I smiled and said nothing, and we soon finished the short walk back to the office. Jones had left, and so had the sun he had been admiring from his window. The unusually warm winter day was replaced by a familiar chill, which made me anxious for my car's heater.

All alone on the drive to Atlanta, the emptiness of spending a holiday away from family and friends sunk in. I hoped talking to my relatives and Christine the next day would alleviate some of that, but of course it wouldn't. Hearing their voices was only going to make it worse. But I had promised to call, so I was just going to do what the assistant warden did when talking to the inmate: wear a smile for the world, and keep my feelings to myself.

There was a Red Roof Inn near the Atlanta airport, about 20 minutes from the city. I decided to check in and make myself at home for the next four or so days. I had interviews to prepare for, and sights to see. This was going to be my vacation. I was going to try to have some fun.

Before then, I had never given holidays much thought. I always took them for granted. It was something that was always supposed to be there, no matter what. Sometimes we celebrate holidays with family and friends, regardless of whether we have a valid reason. And sometimes, we sleep in a hotel on the outskirts of Atlanta, with nothing but melting ice cubes and our thoughts to keep us company.

I was very aware of all the imprisoned men and women who would also be spending this Thanksgiving away from home. Some would never spend a holiday with their families again.

CHAPTER 7

AN EMPTY CUP

"A white guy in Mississippi bit a black woman 72 times and didn't get death. But if the same thing happened to a white woman, it would be all over."
—Clive Smith, Southern Prisoners Defense Fund

"Once they get into a client's case, the lawyers will be appalled by the misbehavior of the prosecution or the ineptitude of the defense lawyer."
—Patsy Morris, Georgia Appellate Resource Center

Atlanta is one of the greatest cities on Earth. I love Atlanta. It has culture, history, and class. It has CNN, the Carter Center and it's the home of Martin Luther King Jr. In 1996 it is going to host the Olympic Games.

It also has the death penalty, which is nothing out of the ordinary for the South. But Atlanta — actually the state of Georgia — is different when it comes to capital punishment. The two most famous legal decisions came out of this state.

The first was the landmark 1972 U.S. Supreme Court ruling in Furman v. Georgia, which declared the death penalty unconstitutional. For abolitionists, it was one of the state's shining moments. Four years later, Georgia made national news again, this time in Gregg v. Georgia. In that case, the Supreme Court set new guidelines under which states could carry out executions. The state that abolished capital punishment had now brought it back. Florida was the first state to rewrite its death penalty laws after the Furman decision.

The top four death penalty states, in number of executions, are Texas, Florida, Louisiana and Georgia, according to the National Association for the Advancement of Colored People Legal Defense Fund. Of the 2800 people sentenced to die in this country since 1976, half are in Southern prisons, and about 200, or 85 per cent, have been executed in the South. California, Pennsylvania, Illinois, Ohio and Oklahoma have sentenced more people to die than every state except Texas and Florida — California has the highest death row population — but have executed a total of only five people (as of May, 1994). During just one 10-week span in 1987, Louisiana executed eight men, Georgia four and Texas three. Atlanta sometimes downplays its political and sociological fraternity with its Southern neighbors, but there's nothing more revealing than the truth.

It was into this world that Clive Smith stepped many years ago after graduating from Columbia Law School. He was born and raised in England, where capital punishment long has been abolished. He is young, in his early 30s, though his work has aged him. He is perhaps most well known for his appearance in a 1987 BBC documentary entitled *14 Days in May* which chronicled the final hours of one of Clive's clients, Edward Earl Johnson.

But it was Clive, not his client, who evoked the most emotion in that film. The pain of capital punishment was etched clearly on Clive's face. It could not have been feigned by even the finest of actors.

The documentary was my first introduction to Clive. As the head of the Southern Prisoners Defense Fund, which handles trials as well as appeals for inmates who can't afford competent counsel, he is considered a leader among his colleagues — for his compassion and his competence.

I had made arrangements to meet with Clive first thing in the morning on the day after Thanksgiving. In the meantime, however, I had to make it through the holiday without getting homesick. My Thanksgiving consisted of walking around an empty shopping mall, seeing a movie, and going back to my motel room for servings of football and tuna sandwiches.

I called Christine during half time which only made me lonelier. Her voice was tired, like mine. I could hear the family in the background, the busy bodies in the kitchen and the kids tearing up the living room. I felt bad because I knew my being away made her unhappy. I had to be here and she had to be there and we hated it.

"Come back soon," she said above the noise of the carving knife.

"As soon as I can," I said.

Half time was over. Thankfully, time, like holiday cheer, is fleeting, and I feel asleep in the glow of the television and to the rumble of the nearby airport.

Clive Smith's house would be considered modest even by middle-class standards. It is a cozy two-story just a mile or two from the heart of Downtown Atlanta. The homes and streets didn't look dirty, just very lived-in. Clive was smiling when he opened the door, but not because of me.

"Did you hear?" Clive said with a wry grin that was part happy and part smug. "Thatcher resigned. I've been waiting for this moment for years!"

I did my best to oblige his enthusiasm, and calm him down for the task at hand. With Bob Dylan droning in the background — an odd selection, I thought, for an Englishman living in the Deep South — we sat with some tea and talked first about his reason for being here, the Southern Prisoners Defense Fund.

The Fund handles cases throughout the Southeast region, stretching as far north as Virginia. The grossly underpaid lawyers survive predominantly on charitable donations and sheer will.

"For every hour we spend on a case, we lose $25," Clive said, his English manner making the statement sound routine rather than unfair. "The prosecution, though, has pretty much endless resources.

"There's a saying about Mississippi: 'The only people who take death penalty cases are students and the town drunk.' It's almost true. I represented a guy there on appeal who was represented on trial by a third-year law student. His first words to the judge were, 'Your Honor, may I have a few minutes to compose myself? I've never been in a courtroom before.' The whole thing can be absurd. The system is rotten from the start, and we're so overworked, we just can't do what needs to be done."

Clive's bitterness is not without reason; he has seen a lot in his handful of years. And he sees no way to make the system any better than it is now.

"You can't have a death penalty system that's fair," Clive said. "If you give to the defense what you give to the prosecution, you'll bankrupt the whole country. This is the only system where one elected official, usually a white male, decides whether to seek death. A guy in Mississippi bit a black woman 72 times and didn't get death. But if the same thing happened to a white woman, it would be all over. There are so many flaws in the system.

"But the ultimate question to me is not the flaws," he said. "Of course there's going to be flaws because it's run by humans. But the ultimate question is: Why bother? I don't know a prosecutor anymore in the South who has even pretended that the death penalty is a deterrent. I respect people who say they are doing it because of vengeance — at least they're being honest. But just jumping up and down and saying you're going to fry people isn't going to solve the world's problems."

The Dylan tape had finished and Clive got up to put on the other side. A death penalty lawyer's life is so stressful, apparently even Bob Dylan's voice can be relaxing.

Despite his cynicism, Clive said he believes the death penalty will be abolished again. Not a temporary stay like Furman provided, but for good, although probably not in his lifetime. Clive said the main problem is what he calls America's "ridiculous political system." Because they pander to public opinion polls, he said, most politicians don't do what's right, but rather what will gain them popularity.

He feels that the best way to eliminate the death penalty, however, is to let the jury see and feel what they are doing — that they are condemning not just a killer, but a human being.

"If I were allowed to sit my client in the jury room to talk to the jurors, I would do it, even if he was guilty as sin," he said. "The humanization of the individual is what we try to do all the time."

That's what Clive tried to do for Edward Johnson, but it was too late. Although Clive had known Edward for years — he knows everyone on Mississippi's Death Row, where Johnson was executed — it wasn't until three weeks before the execution that Clive took up the case.

Edward, who was black, was 18 when he was tried and convicted in 1979 for murdering a white police officer and assaulting an elderly white woman. His trial lawyers never went to the scene of the crime, missed the pre-trial hearing and had no funds to conduct an independent investigation. For the next eight years, he was represented by a lawyer with no capital punishment experience.

Clive took the case after Edward lost his first Constitutional appeal. One week later the documentary camera crew from England arrived, and Clive began the most excruciating ordeal of his career.

"I had never lost a case up to that point, and I was absolutely certain we were going to win this," Clive said, adding that it's still hard to relive the memory of that time. "He was just a decent guy, and I had real doubts as to whether he committed the crime.

"But we kept getting closer and closer to the execution," he said. "We lost in District Court, and when we went to file an appeal in the Fifth U.S. Circuit Court, they were already writing the opinion (to deny).

"Those people are so jaded, particularly some judges," Clive said softly, his voice dripping with contempt. "They've stopped seeing what's going on around them."

Clive continued with Edward's story. "One day, very near the execution, I was watching television with Edward, and they were polling people about the execution. One woman said he shouldn't be killed, and that there were some real doubts to his guilt. Another guy said, "Yeah, yeah, kill him, he should have been dead years ago." It was just like being in a Roman amphitheater, with people putting their thumbs down, and I really wondered if the world had gone anywhere in 2,000 years."

Clive said none of the guards at the Mississippi prison thought the execution should occur, which gave him some comfort. Some of them cried during the execution and resigned afterward in protest. Even in the 11th hour, Clive still held out hope that the Supreme Court would intervene with a stay. Clive's greatest source of comfort, however, was Edward himself.

"Edward spent his whole time comforting me," Clive said. "Having the BBC people around was helpful, too, because they injected an air of total unreality. You kept waiting for someone to yell 'cut', and that would be the end of the movie.

"The night Edward was killed, I went into the execution chamber, and his last words to me were, 'Is there something you know that I don't?' He thought I knew something about how we were going to get this stopped. And all along, I hadn't told him the truth — that there was no hope.

"After five minutes, he finally said, 'Let's get it over with.' I felt completely powerless and helpless to do anything to stop it."

Clive's sadness and depression over the execution quickly turned to anger when he listened to a news media reporter describe how "easy" the execution was, and noted in detail the remains of Edward's shrimp dinner. It makes him angry still.

"It's a pagan ritual, it really is," Clive said about executions. "It's like being among a bunch of druids, like when they're getting ready to sacrifice some virgin to a non-existent god. It's exactly the same. They have to go through all these rituals, because they have to depersonalize it — otherwise, they wouldn't be able to go through with it.

"You sit there thinking, 'Is there nothing I can do to stop this?' It is all so unreal. And then they sacrifice the individual to the false god of deterrence, to the god of politics.

"They would never do it to me," he added, that slight, wry smile returning to his lips. "I'm not black, I'm not poor, and I'm much too well educated."

Clive couldn't sit still any longer. He had to get to that newspaper and revel in Margaret Thatcher's demise. Even a man of compassion like Clive Smith can take pleasure in the foibles of others.

Before he said good-bye, Clive pointed me in the direction of the Martin Luther King Center for Nonviolence. I was here as a journalist, but I was also a tourist, and there still was much I wanted to see.

I almost drove past the MLK complex at first. I was looking for some big monument, a large building that would stand out on any city street; but it was nothing like that. The MLK Center blends in with the rest of the city, and sits adjacent to the Ebeneezer Baptist Church where it all began for the young Dr. King — a place rich in history if nothing else.

King's grave lies between the Center and the Church, surrounded by flowers and a reflecting pool. The sounds of nearby cars and other sounds of city life fall silent when you look at the resting place and the "free at last" lines from the epitaph. Would there still be a death penalty if King had survived the '60s? Maybe so, but perhaps the end would now be in sight. There lay a man, I thought, who changed an entire nation and sent shock waves throughout the world without lifting a finger in violence. Yet we are a nation that feels it must murder its own citizens to bring peace to its streets.

Maybe that's why people still sing "We Shall Overcome". We have such a long way to go.

I got in more than enough sightseeing over the holiday weekend. I visited the Carter Center, went shopping for nothing in particular, and paid a visit to that media mega-giant, CNN. I had seen the old complex years ago, before Ted Turner bought the tallest skyscraper he could find and became the biggest figure in mass media since Joseph Pulitzer. Like many middle-class Americans, I am so sickened by gluttonous greedheads such as Turner that I'll spend $10 on a half-hour tour just so I can take pictures and buy souvenirs of all the things I hate. That should teach him a thing or two.

The tour wasn't the most eye-opening experience of the day. That honor goes to the homeless man who approached me in the CNN Center lobby, not for money, but for conversation.

"Where are you from?" The question came out of nowhere, as did the man. He looked 40ish, wearing a purple long-sleeved shirt, a green jacket-vest, a black hat, and a beard grown more by neglect than purpose. As we talked, he would continuously sip from an empty styrofoam cup. I wanted to tell him there was nothing in there, although I'm sure he knew. I just stared at the cup, rising and falling from the man's lips with mechanical precision.

I'm not sure what the cup had in it before it was empty, but as we talked, I got the feeling it was more likely vodka than coffee. We talked about life on the streets, and how being homeless is a lot like being in prison — except that in prison you get three meals a day and a warm place to sleep. But that wasn't the worst part.

"It's the loneliness," he said, taking another imaginary sip. "All the time, loneliness. All of my friends are dead or gone."

I was going to tell him how lonely I felt on Thanksgiving, but decided against it. Here was a guy who has endured the same ugly feeling for six years, and I was depressed about one day spent in a warm hotel room, with the people I loved just a phone call away. His cup was empty, but my cup runneth over.

There was one other thing he said which struck me as odd, yet painfully true.

"The day after Christmas," declared this street-wise Socrates, "a business is made or broken by how well it does the day after Christmas. Everything is defined by where you are the day after Christmas."

We had been talking about Thanksgiving, but I wasn't going to argue. This was his conversation. I was just along for the ride. I gave him some money as I got up to take my tour, which he accepted, but I don't think expected. When I came downstairs an hour later, I saw my friend talking to a couple of other street people, and he waved at me as I passed.

He still had his cup, and it was just as empty. And I felt bad, really bad, because I knew that on the day after Christmas, he would still be there.

That evening I prepared for my interview the next day with Patsy Morris of the Georgia Appellate Center, and plotted my route back to Alabama for another round of death penalty discussions. The homeless man — I kicked myself for not writing down his name — was still on my mind, however.

I thought about a drive I took during the fall campaign season with the director of a Democratic Party Political Action Committee. We were traveling through Oxnard, the largest city in Ventura County, California, when we saw a homeless person crossing the street.

"Do you see that?" said my companion. "That's the GOP's fault. We have the Republicans to thank for that."

I had to agree with that statement; in a way, trickle-down economics had just been a metaphor for urinating on the under-privileged. But she was also wrong. We are all responsible for what happens to each other. Just because one group starts doing something wrong doesn't mean another group has to stop doing what is right.

When someone is executed, the blood stains everyone's hands. And when someone goes hungry, there should be a pang in ever stomach. To forget this would be less than humane, but, unfortunately, all too human. Still a long way to go.

The bright morning sun and the challenge of a new week helped wipe the sleep from my eyes. My love for this city remained, but it was time to move on.

Before I could do that, however, I had to make it through lunch with Patsy Morris. It's not that I wasn't looking forward to our meeting, it's just that from what I had heard, Patsy was a chain smoker with unusual eating habits.

I packed my car for the afternoon drive to Alabama, and then headed back into downtown Atlanta for the last time. The jewel of the South I thought — or more like a diamond in the rough.

The Georgia Appellate Resource Center sounds a lot nicer than it looks. The small, one-story building was in dire need of a face-lift, or at least a vacuum cleaner. Bodies and paper were flying everywhere, a mad frenzy of committed, breathless, and under-financed activity.

In the eye of this legal hurricane sat 60ish Patsy Morris, her thin strands of gray hair and frail body nearly hidden by the clutter. She was wearing a long-sleeved shirt, a blue skirt and penny loafers, and stopped sucking her Betty Davis cigarette holder long enough to cough "hello". The tiny office was a monument to mess and to the death penalty. Framed articles on important cases hung on the walls, along with pictures of inmates such as John Spenkelink from Florida. One framed picture was an editorial cartoon from the *Atlanta Constitution*, depicting a smiling judge above a podium overlooking two doors. The door leading to a normal jail cell said "white". The door leading to the electric chair said "colored".

Sadly, Patsy's life is no cartoon; her struggle is real. When she takes a case, the door to the electric chair is already open. Maybe the chain smoking is understandable.

Patsy insisted we walk to a restaurant that was a good 10 blocks away. I didn't mind, it's just that by the time we arrived, I was nearly out of breath trying to keep pace.

Patsy ordered what she told me was her usual, which I believed since she didn't even look at the menu: a hamburger, "very rare", and a Bloody Mary. Oh yes, and an ashtray.

With the din of a Yuppie lunch crowd and a leafblower blaring through my skull, I learned that Patsy's job primarily is to recruit volunteer lawyers to take death cases, and provide them with all the research and instruction they need. She's not a lawyer, though she claims she knows more about capital punishment than most lawyers do.

"When Furman came down in 1972, there was a lot of hope that that was it," said Patsy, who previously worked for the Georgia American Civil Liberties Union. "But the states immediately began passing new laws, and on March 28, 1973, Georgia had its new law.

"There was a general consensus that as cases started being affirmed under these new laws, lawyers had to be found for the appeals," she said. "I just started doing it. We needed volunteers because mandatory U.S. Supreme Court review was part of the new laws, and there were no guarantees of representation after the initial appeal.

"I never ask volunteers their personal views on the death penalty," Patsy said, biting into her bleeding entree. "It's none of my business. If they are willing to take a case and do a good job, then what they think about the death penalty isn't particularly relevant. Besides, once they get into a client's case, the lawyer will be appalled by the misbehavior of the prosecution or the ineptitude of the defense lawyer."

Patsy has another role besides counseling legal counsel. She also is a friend and advisor to the residents of Death Row and the forgotten victims — their families. She has been through countless executions, though she has never witnessed one.

"God forbid, I would never ask," she said, lighting another cigarette. "I can't imagine anything sicker than to willingly want to witness someone being killed. The whole concept of the state taking someone's life in my name is so repulsive.

"Prison officials are lying through their teeth when they try to rationalize their participation in the taking of a human life. Why don't we know who throws the switch? Because no one wants the responsibility of throwing the switch. I think there are some people in the prison business who are as amoral as some people on Death Row."

Dealing with the effects of an execution are bad enough without having to watch one, she said. The process and outcome can be debilitating.

"You don't know if you can keep doing your work or not," Patsy said as we got up for the long walk back. "You never know until you go through an execution. But most people who have been doing this work for any length of time have found that they can continue. Their obligations are to the people who aren't dead.

"The thing about executions that's different about dying is that only in an execution context do you have to sit and wait for The Minute. When someone is dying, you don't know the actual moment when death will come. In an execution you do. The clock is just horrible."

I asked her if she ever got angry. Patsy took a long drag on her cigarette, exhaled into the cool Atlanta air and answered slowly, deliberately.

"Anger is a very useless, debilitating, hateful emotion," she said. "Dealing with the grieving while also dealing with the anger takes three times as long."

With that we parted; Patsy returned to her rumpled office, and I returned to my cramped car and searched for my map. She had work to do, and so did I.

I found the best route to Alabama and started out. My destination was Limestone County in the northern part of Alabama, which was too far to get to by nightfall. I decided to drive easy, and try to enjoy the scenery and serenity of the American South.

The highway rumbled with light traffic as I left Atlanta, the shiny CNN Center glimmering in my rear view mirror. This is still the city of Ted Turner, peach trees, Martin Luther King and Jimmy Carter, I thought.

But it is also the city where faded men with tired smiles sip hope from empty styrofoam cups, waiting for the day after Christmas to set them free at last, free at last.

CHAPTER 8

A DAY'S WORK

"Not everybody on Death Row needs to be executed to keep society safe."
—J.D. White, former Death Row warden

"If you ask me if it's more likely that a poor person will go to the electric chair than a wealthy person, then I'll say yes, every time. Poor people are also more likely not to have good teeth. It's not fair, but life's not fair."
—Alabama prosecutor Jimmy Fry

When I woke up, the following sentence was replaying itself in my head: There are no reformed criminals in the South, only dead ones.

I had stayed at the Cullman Days Inn motel, which is somewhere in northern Alabama. When you think about it, though, there's not much that's northern about Alabama at all. This is especially true here, away from the cities. This is, as they say in the old movies, "Every Yankee For Himself" country.

I was beginning to feel like the South was industriously handing out wholesale death sentences. But surely not every prosecutor, DA and warden eagerly sanctioned human slaughter. I thought Charlie Jones was that way, but he proved me wrong.

I wasn't so sure, however, about the man I was about to meet. J.D. White was the warden at Holman for the first execution in Alabama since reinstatement, arguably the most brutal in the state's history. He hasn't discussed the execution with the media since that day on April 22, 1983, which made me even more curious about what really happened to John Evans.

I didn't know much about John, who was convicted of killing a Mobile, Alabama pawn broker, but I knew enough to understand it was not a typical execution. A United Press International reporter who witnessed the event described it this way:

Warden J.D. White pulled the switch and sent 1,900 volts burning into Evans, who clenched his fists and arched his body rigidly into the retaining straps. A moment later, as spark and flame crackled around Evans' head and shaven, razor-nicked leg, white smoke seeped from beneath the veil and curled from his head and leg. Midway through the surge of electricity his body quivered, then fell back into the chair as the current ended.

We thought that was it...two doctors filed out of the witness room to examine the body and pronounce Evans dead. The prison doctor placed a red stethoscope to (Evans), turned and nodded, the natural sign for "Yes, he's dead." But the nod meant he had found a heartbeat. The other doctor confirmed...

They left the chamber and a guard reattached the power lines to the chair and the electrode that fell away when a leg strap burned through. Evans' chest rose against the straps the first time. It rose evenly once, twice, maybe again. A stream of saliva ran down the front of his white, prison smock...I strained to figure out if this was convulsive movement in Evans' strap-crossed chest, and concluded absolutely not. This was slow, deep breathing...

Spark and flame accompanied the onset of the second charge, but this time, for a grim second, the veil slipped a fraction of an inch on the left side, giving the impression it was burning through and would fall away, exposing his face....

When the second charge subsided, the doctors reexamined Evans and again it was clear they found a pulsating heart. A third charge was administered, and the doctors went back for a third time...I seriously thought they would have to bring in a gun and shoot Evans...

John Evans finally was pronounced dead after the third cycle, amid pleas for clemency and a futile appeal to the governor.

Through it all, White was the man in charge, overseeing the pulling of the switch once, and again, and again.

In his book, Joe Ingle describes John Evans as a kind and gentle man who regretted his crime. I would expect as much from someone like Joe, who finds good in almost anybody. I was surprised, however, at his impression of White: "I liked the man," Joe wrote. " He was personable and had been cooperative as possible in honoring John Evans' wishes."

So the questions for me remained: Who is J.D. White? And would he tell me what happened the night John Evans was killed? The answers, I hoped, lay ahead, beyond the large iron gate of the medium security Limestone Correctional Center.

Limestone was different than the other prisons I had visited so far. There were no high walls, no lurking guards to disarm me of my camera or bark at me from a cement perch.

But like the other prisons, this one also was hard to find. The directions I got from J.D. White's secretary said to go past the Baptist church, down a hill, past the creek and over the bridge, and then take the first left — you can't miss it. I missed it. I turned left at the wrong creek.

When I finally arrived, the first thing I noticed when I parked my car was a dark blue pickup in the spot marked "Warden". A sticker on the rear bumper read: "If it ain't country, it ain't music."

J.D. White certainly looked like country. A big man with a big smile, and a monster of a handshake, White told me he was the warden at Holman from December 1980 to July 1984. He began his career at Holman as an entry-level line officer, and like Charlie Jones, quickly worked his way through the ranks. Although he didn't request it, White said he welcomed the transfer to Limestone in 1984.

"We've got everything here," White said, as if with the pride of ownership. "We've got murderers, rapists, white collar criminals, everything. But this is much easier than in Atmore."

What made Atmore difficult, he said, was the death penalty. He said he had to sit down and search his soul — and the Bible — before ultimately deciding he could take the job.

"It took me a month, month and a half," White said. "I talked to several ministers and religious counselors, and they pointed out various scriptures in the Bible that, um, if you want to use this as justification or relief as evidence that you are not committing any crime or a sin, then here it is."

What about the other side, I asked, such as "Thou shalt not kill" and "Turn the other cheek?"

"You can get different approaches to anything from the Scriptures," he answered.

White said that overall he was proud of what he accomplished at Holman, including group exercise programs and liberal visitation policies. But he admitted that he is most remembered for April 22, 1983.

Some say John Evans was tortured; other say he never felt a thing. For more than seven years, J.D. White hasn't said much of anything. It took about 10 minutes of convincing, but ultimately White agreed to talk about what happened that April night. Perhaps I seemed honest. Maybe it was just time for him to talk. In any case, he talked — and I listened.

"Evans was the first execution since reinstatement of the death penalty," he said, speaking slowly and thoughtfully. "Naturally, all kinds of things are going through your mind. We had a lot of protesters that night, both pro and con. But there was no violent reaction.

"We practiced for a couple months before the execution. We had volunteer officers resist, faint, do everything we thought this man might do. I even timed myself on how long it would take to read the death warrant. We had all this stuff timed out, and the only thing we didn't have timed out was knowing what the inmate's specific reaction was going to be. As it was, he presented no problem whatsoever. He walked into the chair with no resistance at all.

"Evans was given three surges. I have heard of cases where the guy was given 13 surges, but we did have an equipment malfunction on Evans. The leg strap on his left leg burned into him on the first surge, and we had to refasten that.

"I knew he was dead on the first surge, but the doctors hadn't officially pronounced him dead. The doctors were too excited. Their skills are in saving lives, and here they were assisting in the taking of a life. They had to rectify that, and they just got excited.

"I didn't have any qualms with it whatsoever as far as executing the man," said White, leaning forward and looking into my eyes. "I was carrying out my job, as a law enforcement officer and as a warden. Of course, I knew a lot more about this Johnny Evans than the average Joe Blow citizen. He was a very cocky guy. He and another guy robbed and murdered a pawn shop broker in the presence of his daughters, shot him in the back. Evans told me, 'Well, I'm confident I'm going to beat this electric chair. I know I'll wind up with life without parole, and then I'm gonna escape, or you're gonna kill me in the process. I've got plenty of time, and I know I'm gonna beat ya. And when I beat ya, the crime spree that put me here is nothing compared to what you're gonna hear about.'

"There were 15-18 different violent crimes these guys did in other states," White said, adding that John's accomplice was executed later under Charlie Jones' watch. "The only time Evans acted like there was a remote possibility that he was going to go to the electric chair was when I went down and told him that the stay had been lifted and the execution was back on.

"He turned ghostly white. He turned around and vomited his stomach up. That was the only indication I ever had from the man that he felt he was going to be executed.

"His father was dead. I met a mother, a sister and a younger brother, and they were as fine a people as I've ever met in my life. The mother was retired, the sister was an educator and the brother was in the CIA. It was a total contrast to John. He definitely was the black sheep of the family.

"They thanked me for being so nice to John over the years, and didn't blame me for anything. They blamed John Louis Evans III. His mama told me that when John was a small boy, his daddy took him hunting, and he killed an animal, a rabbit or squirrel. He liked it, so he started killing the animals around the house — the dogs, the chickens, the cats. They spent hundreds of thousands of dollars on therapy for him, but he just liked violence. In my opinion, they were finally relieved."

Despite the eyewitness accounts, White still believes that John Evans felt no pain during any of Yellow Mama's three surges.

"Electrocution is faster than the speed of light," he said. "Just boom, that's it. I don't challenge the fact that there's smoke at times in executions, but he can't feel a thing. I did have some thoughts when Evans was placed on a stretcher just after his execution, that just a few minutes ago this guy was alive, but that was it. I wouldn't say it was a shocking thought."

White obviously felt John Evans got what he deserved. But he wavered on whether everyone on Death Row deserves to suffer the same fate.

"As a practical matter, I don't know of anyone on Death Row who was innocent of a crime, or didn't deserve to be there," White said. "But not everybody on Death Row needs to be executed to keep society safe. I'm thinking mostly of the older inmates. Perhaps more consideration should be given to the elderly under the death penalty.

"But you never know," he quickly added. "I can't predict behavior, even if I've known someone for 40 years. I see the death penalty as a deterrent to violent crime, but we're not using a golden opportunity to deter crime greater than we already are. There is no such thing in our country as swift and sure punishment. We have the best system in the world, but no swift or sure punishment.

"Also, we tend to perform executions quietly and behind closed doors, and I think it should be a public affair, for the deterrent effect. Rather than having one location in the state, I think the execution should be performed in the county where the crime was committed and the man was found guilty. I don't think it should be televised, but I think it should be announced and done publicly."

We had been talking for almost two hours, until finally it was time for White to get on with his daily routine. I thanked him and walked back through the iron gate to my car and the short drive to Athens for my meeting with prosecutor Jimmy Fry.

As I drove away, my mind still replaying White's comments on public execution and his emotionless recounting of John Evans' execution, I continued to hear: There are no reformed criminals in the South, only dead ones.

I was looking forward to meeting Jimmy Fry. His surname befit his reputation: five murder cases, five victories. He was the master of the legal long ball and he was batting a thousand. He was re-elected in 1988 to another six-year term without opposition.

I arrived in Athens during business hours, but the streets were as quiet as a Sunday afternoon. It didn't seem the place where high-powered attorneys make life-and-death decisions.

I parked in front of the Limestone County Courthouse, my car in the shade of a monument "To the Confederate Soldiers of Limestone County." I walked closer to see the inscription which read: "Ennobled by Triumph, Exalted by Defeat." It seems every town in this part of the country has a Civil War memorial — not for hatred's sake but for history's.

I only had to wait a few minutes before a portly man with cropped black hair invited me into his office. His manner was warm and unassuming, a marked change from the careful wardens I had met.

We joked about his surname, a ribbing which Fry took good-naturedly. He assured me he wasn't as bloodthirsty as his name might imply, though he admitted that, despite the teachings of his church, the death penalty was something he always favored.

"I'm a typical Southern conservative, so there are some things you generally believe in, and the death penalty is one of them," said Fry, who has a painting of Washington crossing the Delaware hanging over his desk. "I believe in the effectiveness of it. I believe in efficiency.

"I grew up in the Methodist Church, which is against the death penalty. I had to struggle with that, and I did, but my mind tells me that there are some things you can do in life which basically forfeit your right to live with other people. Life is not a free ride; we have to pay as we go.

"There is a value in the death penalty," Fry said. "For most law-abiding citizens, it reinforces positively that something bad does happen to people who do bad things. We need to know that there is some order in the world, and I really think the death penalty is a deterrent. But it's not very cost-effective," Fry conceded. "We probably spent a million on Thomas."

"Thomas" is Kenny Thomas, the first person Fry sent to Death Row; (of the five murder convictions, he's obtained a verdict of death only once.) The case hit Fry somewhat close to home, as the victim, an 82-year-old woman, was the grandmother of a close friend.

"It was a very atrocious case," Fry said. "Thomas broke into her mobile home, burglarized it, and then raped and sodomized the woman. He mutilated her with a knife, and did some very animalistic things. He tried to set the home on fire but was arrested at the scene.

"He admitted to the crime and we had all kinds of evidence, including fingerprints in blood," he said. "The entire trial took about two weeks, and it was the longest death case we ever had around here.

"It was a very stressful trial," Fry said. "I asked people to pray for me, and I prayed that the Lord would give me the strength and courage to do what's right and bring the truth out. I was filled with the power of a presence, and a calmness.

"It was an enormous thing, putting a guy to death," Fry said, adding that the Thomas case was the county's first death case in 23 years. "It was a very significant spiritual event in my life; it was real.

"You know something?" Fry said. "I could pull the switch if I had to. I could take him out into the square and shoot him if that were the law. I wouldn't enjoy it — I don't get paid to hate anybody — but I would do it.

"I'm sure Thomas' death will have an effect on me," Fry said. "I want to witness it. I feel morally responsible because I put the guy there. It will be a test of my own conviction."

Fry made no mistake about his views toward Kenny Thomas. This was someone who not only deserved to die, but needed to. Jimmy Fry, however, is not a shark stimulated by the smell of blood. There have been cases, he said, when he decided death was not a justifiable end. Murder is murder, he admitted, but death is different. There are certain rules and specific guidelines to follow.

"The death sentence is not a game," Fry said. "When (Thomas) dies, I will have been just like an executioner. I have got to be able to live with that, so I've got to be pretty damn sure I'm right, and I've got to be pretty damn sure in my own mind that what I'm doing is the right thing. If someone goes after the death penalty just as a matter of policy, then in my opinion that's more outrageous.

"Sometimes the public cries for things it doesn't really want," Fry said. "In Alabama, I'm sure 70 percent of the people are for the death penalty, but at the same time, if I could sit down and talk with them like you and I are talking right now, then they probably would agree that death shouldn't be the first thought as far as a punishment is concerned. Most DA's, for that matter, wouldn't go after a death sentence just because it may be politically popular.

"The death penalty is not something to be glib about," Fry said. "It's as serious as it gets. We've been executing people here for a long time, and it's a terrible, horrible way to die."

Fry agreed that there is a certain amount of discrimination against poor people when it comes to the death penalty.

"Poor people in this country don't receive the same services as everybody else," he said. "It doesn't mean the courts are bad, it's just an economic fact. The system bends over backwards to see that the least of our citizens receive the best possible defense, but you could always say, 'If I had a better attorney...' The legal question is not the best representation, but adequate representation.

"If you ask me if it's more likely that a poor person will go to the electric chair than a wealthy person, then I'll say yes, every time. Poor people are also more likely not to have good teeth. It's not fair, but life's not fair.

"Thomas had been in a series of foster homes and never did very well in school," Fry said. "He had all kind of problems, and the defense said this fella never had a chance. But I think he had a lot of opportunities to make things better. I still say we're free agents, and that there should be some good in all of us. You can't blame crimes on the way people were brought up."

I asked Fry to expand on his comment that most people in Alabama, though in favor of the death penalty, would at least give it some careful thought. Fry said not everyone in the South is as rabid as they may be portrayed.

"I guess what happened at the Bundy execution was human instinct, an eye for an eye," Fry said. "But I don't think the general public attitude is reflected by those who attended the execution. To me, that was barbaric.

"The South has always had this Bible Belt image, where punishment is harsh and severe," he said. "There's a lot of ugly stuff about the recent history of the South. I think the South has an image problem, and we tend to promote it.

"I don't know if the death penalty, however, is strictly a Southern tradition. I mean, people out West used to hang folks for stealing horses. My guess is that part of the South's image might have been a backlash against the Supreme Court and federal government telling us what to do, from integration to the 1972 overturning of our death penalty statutes."

In time, Fry said, such discussions about the death penalty may be moot. I wasn't sure if he was trying to end the interview — it was getting late — or if he really meant it. Regardless, Fry said he believes the death penalty is destined to become a punishment of the past.

"My guess is that support for the death penalty will weaken," he said. "People will decide it takes too long, and that it's not the answer to our problems. Not that it's my personal desire, but my hunch is that we will join the rest of the world sometime early in the next century.

"But if all the people on Death Row were killed tomorrow, we would be a safer nation," Fry said, slowly leading me to the door. "It would have a compelling effect on career criminals. It might give them some reason to think about their lifestyle."

With that parting comment, we said good-bye, and within minutes I was back in my car and on the road again. A feeling of accomplishment swept over me as I realized my trip through the Deep South had come to an end. I pulled onto I-65 and headed north, destination Nashville.

It seemed as if it had been an eternity since I arrived in Washington for the death penalty conference and met with Joe Ingle. His voice and his ideas had stayed with me throughout my trip, and had been interwoven with the words of the people I had met. Now I was going to spend some real time with him, and the people to whom he had dedicated his life. It couldn't have been more perfect.

That's why I should have known there were going to be problems when the rain started to fall as I reached Nashville. There was still an hour or so of daylight left, but the sun was hidden by the dark clouds. For some people, rain meant good luck. For me, it only meant that sooner or later, I was going to get wet.

I checked into a motel and drove to a nearby coffee shop. As was usual practice whenever I came to a new town, I bought a copy of the local paper and read it cover to cover. That wasn't necessary to find this story, however. No, this story was on page one, so no one would miss it.

Joe Ingle, twice nominated for the Nobel Peace Prize, wouldn't be going to prisons anymore. For personal and professional reasons, he was calling it quits.

The official explanation, according to the article, was that the Southern Coalition on Jails and Prisons — Joe was the director — had run out of money. Unofficially, however, there was much more to it than that.

Joe, understandably, said he was sick and tired of going to the funerals of friends who had been executed, despite all his efforts to save their lives.

"You fight the death penalty for 17 years and look up and realize it's an evil that's going to continue no matter what you've done, and I've buried 19 of the 146 people killed since that time," a despondent Joe Ingle told The Associated Press.

As far as I knew, our meeting at Tennessee's Death Row was still on for the next morning. But that's not what I was thinking about. I was thinking about Joe's impassioned speech in Washington about his friend Ray Clark. I thought about Ray's execution, and the futility Joe must have felt in being unable to stop it.

I thought about my coffee; it was stone cold. And so was I.

It was pouring by the time I got back to the motel, and it continued for hours. It seemed like it was never going to stop. I needed to get to sleep, but I was still thinking about Joe. Now, however, I was angry. At the people who did this to him; at society; at the world.

When an inmate kills, it's a murder, and when the state kills, it's an execution. It sounds cleaner, more sterile. "Murder" makes us sound responsible. But when the state kills, the blood from that killing is on all of our hands, whereas when an individual kills, the blood is first and foremost on that person's hands.

And the stain, especially the stain from an execution, can't ever be washed away. Not even in a pouring rainstorm in Nashville, Tennessee.

CHAPTER 9

ODE TO JOE

"This is where I am meant to be. To what end, I don't know. But this is where I'm meant to be and whom I am meant to be with."
— Joe Ingle, May 8, 1984.

"It's gut-wrenching stuff to go through and I need a break."
— Joe Ingle, Nov. 25, 1990.

I woke up to that smell. I hadn't smelled it in a long time, not since I was a kid, but I remembered what it was like. After a particularly hard rain, when I finally was allowed to venture outside, the smell would be everywhere. The ground was still damp, but not dangerously so. The angry clouds had called a truce, and the previously invisible sun was busy clearing up the past night's confrontation. It was a safe feeling, like the world and I had just survived a perilous ordeal, and now we were being comforted by the sun's forgiving rays. That was the smell — the scent of renewal, of a beginning from an end.

This morning, however, was absent the sun's grace. The rain of the previous night had left its gray clouds, its sense of imminent danger. It was dark, dreary, and cold. All too appropriate, I thought, for a visit to Tennessee's Death Row. Too appropriate, for sure, on the day of Joe Ingle's last prison visit as head of the Southern Coalition on Jails and Prisons. Judging from the articles I had read the day before, it could be his last visit to a prison ever.

I thought back to when I first met Joe at the Washington death penalty conference. We spoke briefly, about me, him, and the death penalty. His quiet strength impressed me, and by the end of the conversation, we agreed to meet in Nashville and talk to some of his favorite inmates.

The only weakness I saw was when talking about Ray Clark. Joe grew quieter, more introspective when Ray's predicament was brought up. Little did I know how much Ray really meant to him. How difficult it must have been, I thought, to hear about Ray's death from London. Not being allowed to call Ray before his death was even worse.

Still, I thought Joe would get over it. He had been through so many executions before. Surely by now he was used to it.

The newspaper headlines as I arrived in Nashville answered that question for me. Joe Ingle had had enough. He didn't want to see his friends die anymore. He was quitting; his ministry was closing its doors.

I wasn't exactly sure how I should feel. I knew this was going to be an emotional day, but I also knew I couldn't get too caught up in it if I wanted to record the events accurately. My feelings for Joe were real, but my job required some objectivity.

I took a shower, got dressed, packed and checked out of the motel. After grabbing a couple local newspapers, I got in my car and began the 10-minute drive to the prison.

The Riverbend Maximum Security Institution is in west Nashville near an industrial park, just a short drive from my motel. There were smokestacks, some houses, and a junk yard in the distance. I made a left turn into the industrial area, and passed a chemical company, gas station, some factory outlets and a restaurant equipment center. Soon the stores disappeared, a sure sign, I figured, that the prison couldn't be too far off. Prisons almost never occupy the same space as the rest of civilization. They almost always are in a field, its residents allowed only to share the same scenery as the cows and the crickets.

True to form, Riverbend lay directly across from a cow pasture, much like the Florida State Prison. And, as in Virginia, the road to the Tennessee prison came to a dead end.

Riverbend looked more like an office building than a prison. The complex was neat and clean, the signs shiny. If it weren't for the ubiquitous barbed wire, the place could have passed for IBM headquarters.

It was, actually, a technological wonder. Every inch of the facility was under electronic surveillance. With this in mind, I parked my car and made no effort to hide my tape recorder or other tools of my trade. I didn't want to attempt any clandestine interviewing techniques with Big Brother watching.

I walked through the electronically controlled doors into a large reception area with soft blue plastic chairs and some vending machines. I crossed the freshly waxed floor to what looked like the main desk. It was; the stern face of the female guard and the metal detector off to the side gave it away. I told her I was waiting for Joe Ingle, though she knew who I was talking about before I even said his last name. Everyone in Tennessee knows Joe Ingle.

After a few uncomfortable minutes of trying to make small talk, I saw a man in tired blue jeans and a dark blue jacket stroll toward the counter. He forced a smile and shook my hand, and apologized for being late.

"I was held up at the office," he said. "There is a lot of packing to do."

This could not be the same person, I thought, whom I had met in Washington. He still was an unassuming man with a friendly nature and choirboy face. He still spoke with a folksy Southern twang that immediately put you at ease and made you forget that you were speaking to a Nobel Prize nominee. But now his mood was more somber, his smiles bittersweet. He looked worn. He wanted to get this over with.

Before we could proceed, however, there was a slight problem to take care of, namely my camera. The guard said I couldn't bring it inside without prior approval. The warden would have to okay it, and he was tied up in a meeting. Oh well, I thought, at least I tried.

I turned to Joe to tell him it was no big deal. Too late. He was already on the phone.

"This is Joe Ingle. Is the warden in, please?"

I tried to stop him. It was just a camera, for heaven's sake; no need to make a fuss over it. What if the warden decided I shouldn't go to Death Row at all?

There was a pause of at least two minutes. The guard and I exchanged blank stares. Smiling was useless; Joe was stepping all over her authority and she couldn't do a damn thing about it.

Suddenly, Joe began explaining the situation to the warden, who, I later found out, had interrupted his meeting to take the call. Joe then handed the phone to the guard. She listened for about 15 seconds and hung up; then she inspected my camera.

"Okay, you can take it in," she said with a sigh.

I looked at Joe with a smile of thanks as well as apology. "You didn't have to do that," I said.

"Don't worry about it," he replied. "It was no big deal."

Joe and I walked on a small outdoor path from the main building to Death Row. We talked about the status of the death penalty in Tennessee, and about the men I was going to meet. His hands stayed securely in his pockets and we proceeded briskly to lessen the severity of the chill wind.

He told me there were 83 people on Death Row in Tennessee, including one woman housed at another facility. But there hasn't been an execution since 1977, when the death penalty was reinstated, though execution dates continuously are handed down by the courts. According to Joe, a date is issued at each level of appeal, but the date only becomes serious when the appeals run out.

That hasn't happened in Tennessee — at least not yet. If and when it does, the three people we were going to meet could be among the first to sit in the state's electric chair.

Rocky Coker didn't actually kill anybody, but was convicted of conspiring to commit murder. Terry King was convicted of a brutal murder of a young girl. Richard Houston was convicted of murder in the course of a robbery in Clarksville, Tennessee. All of them maintain their innocence.

Joe called the men the "leaders" of Death Row, primarily because they are among its long-time residents. I was cautioned not to discuss their cases, only their feelings. As we walked down the greenbelt path toward Death Row, Joe spoke in measured tones with his eyes cast downward. He didn't have to look up because he knew the way so well. This was natural for him.

In fact, he was so at ease, the realization that we were walking unescorted through a maximum security prison didn't hit me until much later. Civilians aren't allowed to roam around a prison unescorted. Only guards, wardens, and, apparently, Joe Ingle are allowed to do that.

We walked into one of the many small buildings and told the guard who we were there to see. The guard asked Joe about the newspaper stories and wanted to know if they were true, if he really was leaving the coalition.

Joe assured him he was. I then asked Joe if he had a chance to find out how the inmates took the news, and with his eyes still glued to the ground, he said quietly, "nobody is very happy about it." After 17 years of fighting against the death penalty, he looked terribly defeated. It was sad to watch.

But Joe was confident that his visits wouldn't be as needed as they were in the past.

"Leaving these guys is bad," Joe said as we walked into the interview room. "But it's not like I'm abandoning them. They've got my home address and phone number. I haven't changed.

"These guys have rehabilitated themselves," he said. "They are who they are through their own hard work."

The interview room looked like a pediatrician's office. There were rows of small plastic chairs, and in a corner, there was a bookcase filled with children's toys and stuffed animals. This room was reserved for the level A and 1-A inmates, or those with the most privileges. They could visit freely with their families here without a guard. They weren't handcuffed or chained like level

B inmates, or stuck behind glass, like level C prisoners. They had here, it seemed, as much freedom of mobility, mind and spirit as anyone else.

Our guests — actually, *we* were the guests — began to arrive as soon as Joe and I sat down. Rocky was the first, and his firm, quick handshake revealed much about his personality. He seemed like the type who, if he didn't get in the first word, would make sure to get in the last.

Then came Terry, a quieter man who looked more like a boy. He was nervous and sat down quickly, folding his hands in his lap.

Richard was the veteran, a Death Row resident since 1979. He said a quiet hello and sat, using his hands to support his chin. I could tell he was a thinker more than a talker, the kind of person who would speak up only if he had something relevant to say.

Joe gave me the floor and hardly said a word for the next two hours. I guess he figured he had done enough talking already. I

(left to right) Joe Engle, Richard Houston, Terry King, and Rocky Coker, Riverbend Maximum Security Institution, Nashville, Tennessee

first asked them what a typical day was like. That was an easy one to answer.

"Routine," said Terry, pointing the toes of his shiny, white Nike tennis shoes. "I have a job here, data processing. I do that Monday through Friday, from 8:15 in the morning to 3:45 in the afternoon. Then we get two hours of exercise time, but that also depends on what level you are."

"Not everyone has a job," added Rocky, interrupting to make his own forceful point. "You have to be level A or 1-A to be considered for a job. I'm a law clerk." Rocky then went into a tirade about the prison's poor medical care and the staff's general laziness. He told a story about an inmate named Richard Caldwell, who allegedly laid in his cell more than two hours after having a heart attack. Rocky said it was three hours before he was taken to the hospital.

Richard piped up, "The staff has an attitude — they don't give a damn," he said. "Each person's cell has an emergency button that alerts central control. On this particular night, when Caldwell pushed his button, the officer didn't come when he was supposed to. The treatment here is generally good, adequate," Richard added, adjusting his dark blue ski cap. "The majority treat you with respect. They won't stand there and talk crazy to you. It's a mutual thing, a cordial relationship. We have to live here and they have to work here. They know that."

Terry and Rocky weren't willing to give their keepers that much slack.

"The guards and staff were so brainwashed before they got here, and then they found out it was totally different than what they had anticipated," Terry said. "They had us all made out to be a bunch of mad dogs, and we're not about that at all. We're just human beings under a sentence of death."

Anxious to get off the subject of the keepers and the kept, I pursued the death penalty question. Why, I asked, do so many people believe in capital punishment? Rocky, who never let me loose from the stare of his dark, penetrating eyes, said education was the problem.

"I can't blame the public for being scared, but I wish people would get more educated before they decide to put people to death," he said. "If they think they should put us to death for an alleged murder, then they should burn arsonists' homes, and they should rape rapists, and they should rape child molesters; let the punishment fit the crime."

Richard: "When you mention the death penalty, a lot of people think of Charles Manson, even though he doesn't have a death sentence. But he's the worst person ever plastered on the news, so they assume that someone under the death penalty has killed 35 to 40 people. They just react."

"People think this is a country club, that we have it good. But when you're deprived of your freedom and have uncertainty about living...a lot of people think that being on Death Row is a piece of cake, and it's a 24-hour strain. Not just on yourself, but on the families, all around. It's like a cancer that just spreads out.

"We don't condone crime or murder," he said, leaning forward like a college professor about to make a critical point. "Murder is wrong in any sense of the word. But to kill me for supposedly killing someone, what kind of lesson are we teaching? We need to teach kids that they shouldn't kill, not because they might go to prison and be executed, but because killing is wrong. Let's teach that instead."

Rocky, not one to be silent for long, added contemptuously, "In the building where Terry and I work we have a lot of dignitaries come though for tours. We've had some state representatives and judges, and they see us walk around with no restraints, and to see us working there they didn't know that we were Death Row. They are amazed. Now if they've had a picture painted for them that we're monsters, then what does the public think?

"People like excitement," Rocky sighed, leaning back. "And when you talk about putting someone to death, strapping him down and taking his life, people love that. They eat that shit up."

Richard: "The death penalty will be abolished because the public is becoming aware that it's not uniform," he said. "Justice is supposed to be blind, but it's not. About 20,000 people commit murder each year, but there are only about 2,000 people on Death Row. With all the murders we read about, why is there such a small percentage on Death Row?"

Terry had been silent for the past several minutes, deferring to the experience of his older companions. Although I directed most of my questions to the group, I looked at Terry when I asked what went through their minds when they first were sentenced to die.

"I was scared," Terry said quietly, acting more the child now than the hardened criminal. "I just knew Death Row from what I saw in the movies. But when I got here, it just blew my mind as to how the people really are. We're just ordinary human beings who made a mistake or were wrongly convicted. We're just human beings in a very tragic situation...we have a heart.

"I didn't think about Death Row or the people on Death Row until I got here," Terry added. "Their lives didn't concern me. People don't think about it until they're faced with that situation."

I smiled a little when Terry said that. He reminded me of all the questions I fielded from my friends when I told them about my interest in the death penalty. They couldn't understand why I was so interested in a bunch of people who had been discarded by society. "Because they exist," I told my friends. "We can lock them up, even kill them, but we can't ignore them."

For Richard, the hardest part about his sentencing was trying not to cry.

"When they gave the death penalty to me, I didn't know how to react," he said. "But because of ego, I told myself that I wasn't going to let my family see me cry. I was trying to put up a front, and go out like a man.

"Every time you look around you know this is it — Death Row," he continued. "You try not to focus on the bad, but I've been here a good while, so I don't believe in the Easter Bunny and all that kind of stuff. Death is a serious possibility."

Rocky assured me that if the time comes, he will not go to the chair quietly.

"I'm going to tell you this right now," he said, readying for another speech. "If I get to the electric chair, my head is gonna be busted and I'm probably gonna be unconscious because I'm gonna do everything...I'm gonna bite, I'm gonna kick, I'm gonna probably be restrained, but I'm not going to just walk and sit down in the electric chair. I'm not that big a man and anyone who doesn't resist is a fool. Self preservation tells me to resist, because in those three or four minutes that you're resisting, anything can happen.

"I'll never be prepared to die. I love life. I'm gonna fight all the way, no matter what."

Richard stared at his friend during his monologue, both with astonishment and a tinge of sadness — not about the thought of his friend's death, but at the way he expected to die. Richard's attitude was quite different.

"I think if it got down that close, I would try to say my prayers, and make sure I asked for forgiveness for all the things I've done," he said. "I wouldn't waste my time giving the guards the benefit of the doubt, letting them say, 'yeah, we broke him.'

"I don't think a man is judged by the amount of pain he can take. I don't want to die, but I've always tried to be strong, no matter what. I love life like Rocky does, but I want to leave a good memory for my family."

Rocky looked over at Richard and smiled.

"You know how I want to die?" Rocky said, turning toward me. "Old age. If there is life, there is hope."

All three inmates said they had contemplated taking their own lives at least once while in prison. What stopped them, they said, was the possibility that tomorrow might somehow turn out better than today.

"You don't know what tomorrow is going to bring," Richard said. "I have strong family support, and if I killed myself I'd be letting them down. They've suffered through this experience just like I have.

"I had two co-defendants," he continued. "They didn't get the chair and I did. It's a roll of the dice. If any of us would have plea bargained, we wouldn't be here. If I cut a deal, I probably could have been out on the streets today."

I asked the inmates what they would do if they were allowed to walk out the door as free men.

"First, I would go to Mecca," said Richard, who converted to Islam after arriving on Death Row. "Then...I think all of us would be good at educating the youth about this whole system, about how easy it is to get in, and how tough it is to get out. We'll let our experience speak."

Rocky said he would get a job in a law office and work to help Death Row inmates. Terry answered the question more philosophically.

"I was just 21 when I got into this trouble, but I've grown up," he said. "I used to think 70 years was a long time, but now I realize that it's nothing. Life is too short to spend it here, to spend it in any kind of trouble. If you spend just one day locked up and have your freedom taken away from you, then you've lost some very valuable time.

"The world is full of opportunities and you've got to take advantage of them," he said. "It's so wonderful to have your freedom."

Terry's mood had grown more silent and reflective as the interview wore on. He continued searching for words to describe how he felt.

"I've been back to court five or six times, and the emotion that goes through me when I get close to Knoxville is indescribable," he said. "It's hard to hold back the tears, it really is, 'cause you're going back to where you grew up, and you see all these places you used to go, and this is where my family lives, y'know?

"I can't explain it," Terry said, putting his head in his hands. "We can sit here all day, with all due respect, and you could never understand. Even the people who helped put me here I wouldn't wish this upon."

Before I could ask the next question, Joe, who had said little if anything for more than an hour, leaned toward me to deliver one of his heartfelt sermons.

"All of these guys could go back to society today," Joe said. "They're all in programs, improving their lives. For people like that you need to give hope, give them encouragement so they will continue. You don't give hope by saying you're gonna kill them or lock 'em up for life. You give hope by saying okay, make something of your life and we'll let you out of here.

"Prison should be rehabilitation. People may be upset that it doesn't always work like that, but that's what prison should be for. And when I talk about rehabilitation, I'm talking about individuals taking it upon themselves to improve themselves. I'm not talking about the system rehabilitating. These inmates are who they are through their own hard work, but the system needs to provide opportunities."

As our talk came to an end, Rocky, Richard and Terry suddenly realized that this was the last time — at least for a long while — that they were going to see Joe. The preacher and the inmates shook hands, and with that emotionless ritual out of the way, hugged.

I couldn't help but feel like an intruder. Joe again looked somber and depressed. It may have hurt too much to stay in the fight, but it also pained him to say good-bye.

The condemned, the people seemingly with the most to worry about, remained positive. Few bothered to help as much as Joe had helped, and fewer remained friends once the helping was over. He would be missed, for sure, but not forgotten.

"Joe's been coming here ever since I can remember," Richard said while Joe and Rocky embraced. "He's paid his dues."

Indeed he has. A United Church of Christ minister, Joe became the director of the Southern Coalition on Jails and Prisons, not because he applied for the job, but because he created it. And it was because he continued that work in every kind of hardship and cruel circumstance that he was nominated twice for the Nobel Peace Prize.

It all began in 1969 when Joe accepted an invitation to study at the Union Theological Seminary in New York City — in Harlem. Born and raised in North Carolina, he was a true Southerner, and attended the Union Theological Seminary in Richmond, Virginia, before he left the South for the first time to bite the Big Apple.

He spent his first year interning at a church in East Harlem, his first real introduction to life's seedier side. But ministering to the poor didn't faze him. He enjoyed working in the city so much, that for his second-year project, he spent nine months visiting prisoners at the Bronx House of Detention.

That was 1971, the year of the famous riots at Attica. Joe had been impressed with the strength of the inmates and their ability to articulate their demands, and was equally disgusted with the violent melees that followed. Those nine months opened a new world to Joe. He never left it.

He received his master of divinity degree in 1973 and was ordained a minister in the United Church of Christ. By this time he was thoroughly convinced that he needed to work in a prison, and moved to Nashville in 1974 to be with the woman he loved and become the Tennessee director of the Southern Prison Ministry.

Later that year, with Joe's help and vision, the Southern Prison Ministry became the Southern Coalition on Jails and Prisons. Joe remained in Nashville to head that chapter, while sister chapters opened in his native North Carolina, as well as South Carolina, Georgia, Mississippi, and Alabama.

Joe was elected head of the coalition in 1976 — the same year the United States Supreme Court again allowed states to carry out death sentences. Capital punishment became the coalition's top priority, both because of its moral repugnance and the fact that most Death Row prisoners were in the South.

In 1977, Joe protested outside the Utah prison where Gary Gilmore was executed by a firing squad, the first of many who would be executed in the United States in the years to follow. Joe since has endured the executions of 13 inmates — 13 friends — throughout the South. He has held their hands until the final moments; he has met and pleaded with governors to search their souls for compassion; and he has even succeeded in getting the Pope to lobby on behalf of the condemned.

Through his tireless efforts, Joe helped to repeal the death penalty for retarded inmates in Tennessee. For that and his devotion to the denizens of Death Row, he twice was nominated for the Nobel Peace Prize, a commendation usually reserved for players on the world stage, superhuman sorts who free nations and risk death for ideals.

But Joe Ingle is human. By August 1990, his life with death had begun to take its toll.

"There were three inmates that I was close to — Billy Moore in Georgia, Ray Clark in Florida, and Joe Giarratano in Virginia," Joe said. "In late August, Billy had his death warrant signed and I went down there to be with him, and he got clemency. That was absolutely wonderful. I remember I talked with him on the telephone; the clemency hearing was in Atlanta and the prison was about 40 miles away. And I realized after visiting with him and his family and my colleagues who had worked on the case that I didn't have the joy I should have had.

"I couldn't feel anything. I was numb. That was when I realized I couldn't go down and be with Ray. If this was the way I was reacting to a victory, there was clearly no way I could handle losing Ray or Joe."

One week after Ray's execution, Joe tendered his resignation — from the coalition and from Death Row.

Joe had promised to make one more appearance after the visit with the three inmates on Level A. We entered a small room about 50 yards from the main reception area to wait for a new arrival who wanted to talk to Joe. This inmate was a Level B, as evidenced by the cuffs around his wrists and ankles. Two guards escorted him into the room, a dark, lifeless place with barred windows, an old table and rickety wooden chairs. Compared to this guy, Rocky and company were living the good life.

The youth — he was in his early 20's — mostly wanted Joe to help with his appeals. But the news of Joe's departure also was on his mind. He didn't believe it. Like a kid whose favorite baseball player let him down, the inmate's face was etched with the words, "Say it ain't so, Joe."

"So, the office is closing?" he said, in a slow and measured voice.

"Yeah, we ran out of money," Joe replied matter-of-factly.

"Are you relocating?" the inmate asked, refusing to believe what his ears were hearing.

"No, um, I've accepted a fellowship up to Harvard University, so I'm going to study for four months up there, and then I'll be looking for another job," Joe said. "Hopefully I'll be working against the death penalty. My wife and I like Nashville and we hope to stay here."

Those words did little to soothe the inmate's feelings. He seemed upset, but more than that, he looked like he was being abandoned. The old guys might be okay on their own, but the new inmates still needed Joe Ingle.

"Will someone still be here for us?" the inmate asked.

Joe's honesty again got the best of his bedside manner. "No, not anymore," he said. "I'm sorry."

Joe listened to the inmate's concerns for about 10 minutes. He gave him some advice on finding a lawyer, and then stood up to say good-bye. It was almost 1 p.m. The morning had flown by and he was hungry.

Ten years ago he would have gone without eating for hours on end when with an inmate, but today, Joe was hungry. It really was time to go.

We drove back into Nashville and stopped at the Coalition office before grabbing lunch. The place was bare, except for stacks of boxes, some papers on a desk and a telephone answering machine with its light blinking furiously. An employee interrupted her packing to tell Joe that a radio station called for an interview, but Joe told her that it and all the other calls from media and friends would have to wait until he could fill his stomach.

We walked across the downtown Nashville street to the Pancake Pantry, one of Joe's favorite haunts, where asking the waitress for the "usual" really works. They started his order as soon as he walked in; he finished a cup of coffee before I even looked at the menu. He still appeared drained and depressed, but we managed to talk for more than an hour between bites of pancake and sips of coffee.

Although I already knew the answer, I asked the obvious question. I asked him why.

"There are two levels to leaving," Joe said. "One is financial. We don't have the money to run this office — it's that simple. Our board has tried everything possible, but we just can't make ends meet.

"The other states with coalition offices need them more than Tennessee does, anyway. We've made some real strides in this state. We haven't had any executions here and we are not going to have any in the near future. Hopefully, the Tennessee Supreme Court will just throw the death penalty out. So, when you look at it from a Southern perspective, Tennessee is the least of our worries.

"On the personal end of that question...well, there is a tremendous drain and toll exacted in this work, and I'm definitely feeling it." He paused for another sip of coffee, stared at it for a moment as if for moral support, and continued.

"I would like to keep working against the death penalty, but I would like to do it in a different way. I don't have the emotional stamina to go down there with Ray Clark for the last hours of his life, or any of the other folks. That's a personal statement about what I've been doing. It's not a statement at all about whether it needs to be done, or whether the death penalty needs to be fought. That's not it. It's just a personal statement."

As Joe talked, I was reminded of a passage in his book, *Last Rights*, about the execution of John Spenkelink in Florida. Joe worked on John's behalf, and took the inability to stop the execution personally. The part I remembered most was when Joe and a friend were on their way to the Florida State Prison in the middle of the night. Through the crackle of the car radio, Joe learned that John's last-ditch appeal had been denied by a federal appeals court.

Joe had leaned his head out the window and shook the still night, screaming, "Is there no justice? Is there no justice? My God, is there no justice?"

I wondered if, with the benefit of hindsight, he now had an answer to that question.

"Well, yes, there is no justice, that's for sure," Joe said, after thinking for a bit. "In the death penalty, there is no justice. However, I was screaming that to God, so I think ultimately there is justice in the world, but certainly in the administration of the death penalty there isn't any. That's not just an intellectual statement — that's a painful acknowledgment.

"But I do believe the death penalty is going to be abolished in this country. I believe it's not going to be as far off as many people think. What's going to happen eventually, and it's a matter of painful education, is the American people are going to stop this. The reason could be economic or just seeing the futility of things, I don't know. But the people will stop it.

"So I haven't given up. I mean, this is sort of stuck in my craw. The death penalty is part of who I am." Obviously, Joe's realization that he needed to get away from the death penalty didn't happen overnight. He considers that a blessing.

"If I had known then what I know now, I probably wouldn't have done it," he said. "It's like the apostle Paul says, 'You see through a glass darkly.' That's a good thing for me.

"But I think...I felt good about what we were doing, trying to keep people alive. We were doing all we could to keep people alive and to comfort their families. And I really felt an immense sense of gratitude and debt, not only for the folks at the prisons, but for their families and what we went through together. We're bonded, forever.

"I don't think I really understood the depth while I was doing it. When things have to be done, you don't really have time to sit around and figure this stuff out. You just gotta do."

By this time our pancakes had arrived and we decided to give ourselves a break. Joe ate like someone who had been stranded in the desert for weeks without food. In a sense, that was comforting. He ravaged the meal as if it were his first, rather than his last — a feast of renewal; a beginning, not an end.

Joe washed down some pancake with his fourth cup of coffee and told me some more about John Spenkelink, the man who prompted him to scream at God.

"John sent a clear message of everything that was wrong about the death penalty," he said. "I remember saying to some of my Southern Coalition friends that I would never get that close with a death penalty inmate again, because it was so painful when John was killed. Well, that didn't happen. It's not hard to like people on Death Row. They're just like other folks except they're there for having committed or for having been convicted of this crime, and they're poor. But in terms of likability, there's no problem with that at all.

"I haven't met anybody who I haven't had affection for, and that's not to deny that they've done some terrible things. But it's like St. Augustine said: You hate the sin, but you love the sinner. Don't get the person confused with what the deed is. That's a real important thing."

John Spenkelink's execution was the first that Joe fought — the first of many battles he lost. Before he died, John introduced Joe to Ray Clark, whose battle Joe ultimately no longer had the strength to fight. But one thing was clear. No one on this Earth loved Ray more than this quiet preacher from Tennessee.

"One of the hardest things for me to do in my life was...I couldn't go down there to be with Ray. He was very understanding, very affirming, and encouraged me not to come. He told me I couldn't do this, and that he would be all right.

"This morning I talked with the minister who was with Ray before he was killed, and it just stirred up all those emotions and all the love I have for Ray.

"And it was hard," Joe said, trying not to cry. "It was hard. It still is hard.

"One of the things the Minster said over and over again was how much I had meant to Ray, and I know that's true. I just hope that Ray had a glimpse of how much he meant to me, because he was a special fellow, one I was very fond of. I keep calling him a sweet man, and I mean that in a true, pure, nice sense of that word. He was a sweet man, his spirit very gentle.

"It doesn't get any easier. There's no routine to desensitize you." Joe was drained again. He apologized for being so tired, saying that talking about his friends saps much of his energy.

"That's one of the things that separates me from a lot of folks who work against the death penalty," he said after asking for yet another refill. "This is not an issue for me — it's people, people I know. It's faces and names. That's kept me going.

"There are people on Death Row who aren't going to like me," he added, "but that's not what matters. What matters is whether the state is killing people, and that has to be responded to."

The only execution Joe witnessed was that of Willie Darden, a Florida man convicted of murder in the course of a robbery. Joe recounted the March 15, 1988 execution in *Last Rights:*

"The guards tilted Willie's shaved head back against the chair at an uncomfortable angle. With his head held back, a chin strap was fastened around his jaw. Willie winced as it was tightened. Still maintaining eye contact with me, he then did a most extraordinary thing. He winked his left eye at me, lifted his left thumb forward, as if to assure me that he was all right. Then, as they dropped the black mask over his face, he waved good-bye with his left hand, even though his arm was strapped down to the infernal device. I almost lost control."

Joe told me the execution made him more than just sad — it made him angry.

"Willie didn't die, he was killed," Joe said. "That term is the finality of evil; that really describes it. The whole process is so banal and ordinary, commonplace, and so fundamentally evil. It is just absolutely disgusting.

"It's not that there is anything physically appalling or unexpected. It's just what it is. You're in a room watching a human being get exterminated. That's an absolutely awful thing to present.

"The governors are the people who are responsible," he continued, his voice beginning to rise. "I don't blame them in the sense that I am angry with them or hold them personally accountable...they have to deal with their own accountability with the good Lord on all this. But I think their actions are morally wrong, no doubt about it. Killing human beings is morally wrong. The governors are abdicating their responsibility in order to enhance their political careers, and that makes me very angry."

Through all of Joe's internal struggles has been his wife, Becca, and for the past three years, his daughter, Amelia. A nurse in a Nashville hospital, Becca recently had surgery for ovarian cancer, placing more stress on an already emotionally taxed couple. Joe did his best to be there for her. After all, she has always been there for him.

"I could never have done this work without Becca," Joe said. "There were months at a time when I didn't have money, so I couldn't offer her anything. I'm grateful for her support, not to mention all the love and emotion." Joe married for one simple reason — love. The reason for his opposition to capital punishment is just as elementary.

"You're either for killing somebody, or opposed to killing somebody. That's the issue here. Trying to dress it up and put fancy words on it doesn't change the fundamental moral element. When you get down to the foundation, that's what it means to me."

Our check had been sitting on the table for 20 minutes before we finally decided it was time to go. I had become so wrapped up in the conversation that the time sped by; the sun had already begun to fall. I had a long drive ahead, but the last thing I wanted to do was leave that little restaurant.

I turned off the tape recorder and put down my note pad. Now disarmed of my journalistic tools, I told Joe what I had been thinking since that first time we met in Washington.

There are many who fight against the death penalty, but none as honest, none as generous, none as courageous as Joe Ingle. He is not for himself, but for every man.

"I just do it, I guess," Joe said, somewhat shocked at my impromptu assessment. "You don't spend a lot of time thinking about yourself. You're concerned about other people, so that's the focus."

Joe said good-bye to the waitresses and I followed him back to the near-empty Southern Coalition office. Ray had written him a letter the night before his early morning execution, and Joe said he would show it to me as long as I promised not to publish it verbatim. But first, still ignoring the note from the radio station, Joe placed a call to Tom Wicker of the New York Times. He urged the columnist to write something about Joe Giarratano, who at the time still was fighting for his life. Joe was right — this work does get stuck in your craw.

He then showed me the letter, a one-page scrawl that was as well-written as it was to the point. Ray thanked Joe for his kindness and friendship, consoling the consoler by telling him not to worry, that he — Ray — would be okay.

The letter recounted a time in 1988 when, during a visit, Ray asked Joe why he was there. Joe answered, "Because I like you," and for Ray, that response embodied why Joe was so special, and why Joe meant so much to him.

The letter ended not with a tear, but with a smile: "I hope you have a wonderful, prosperous life."

It was such a positive letter, it was hard to feel sad. Then I looked at Joe. His eyes were wet. I suddenly felt an incredible sense of loss. The person who wrote that beautiful letter was dead. And a part of Joe had gone with him.

Joe and I shook hands, and I walked down the five flights of stairs to my road-weary and weather-beaten car. After a quick check of the map, I headed north with the chilly Nashville air sweeping through my open window.

My heart was empty, but my mind was full. I thought about Rocky, and his revelation that some Death Row inmates can be less fortunate than others.

"We complain a lot, but at least we are Level A," he told me with that machine gun voice. "I look at people who come in on level B who have much less privileges than we do, and I realize that, my God, we actually could be worse off that this."

Level B — that inmate we met was so scared, naive, and so sad that the great Joe Ingle wasn't going to be around to help him like he had helped so many others. Rocky was right; this guy was much worse off. Without Joe, he would be alone.

Joe. As the night wore on and the states rolled by, I found fewer and fewer words to describe this man of God, this man for mankind. I told myself — enough times almost to believe it — that he would be back. He would, as he told the crowd in Washington at the abolitionist conference, march into the future knowing he had triumphed, that finally he had beaten the odds.

I thought about a passage from Joe's book where he talks about the concerns of James Adams, one of the many inmates whom he has touched and who, in turn, touched him. This, I decided, was the Joe Ingle I wanted to remember: the man who cared when others couldn't, who worked, lived and breathed in the shadow of death.

"James was concerned about me tonight. He wanted to know if I could keep doing this, keep enduring the awfulness of friends being isolated and killed. I found myself telling him, 'James, I wouldn't want to be anyplace in the world but here tonight. I wouldn't want to do anything but be here with you. This is where I am meant to be. To what end, I don't know. But this is where I'm meant to be and whom I am meant to be with.'"

By nightfall, I was in Illinois. Most of me, anyway.

CHAPTER 10

FROST BITES

"You have seen many lay in these cages and grow old, enduring the suffering and misery, the loneliness, without proper medical treatment, the petty bullshit, the static of all these damn fools and idiots. So it's senseless to lay in one of these cages enduring all that when the end result is still the same — death. As we both know, I'll never see the streets again."

— Charles Walker, in a letter to a former Death Row inmate, on his decision to end his appeals

"There is still this fear that these guys are going to get released, and that is simply not true."
— Walker's attorney, Chuck Sheidel

I had forgotten how cold the Midwest can be. When I pulled into Springfield well after dark, all my tired eyes could see were the lights of a motel and my breath. The gravity of the cold didn't weigh on me until the morning, when my eyes and my senses opened to the chill of winter.

I was still thinking about Nashville. It was cold there, too, and I wondered how Joe Ingle was feeling, and how he slept last night. But as I pulled my weary body into the shower, my thoughts eventually turned to my reason for enduring this late November frost: Charles Walker.

Many famous men came from Illinois. Abraham Lincoln is perhaps the most famous, though who could forget Al Capone or Mayor Richard Daley. Charles Walker is famous, too, but it's the kind of fleeting fame that ultimately will become a speck upon the pages of history. Shortly before I arrived, he became the first person executed in Illinois in more than 28 years. It was the first execution in a northern industrialized state since reinstatement of the death penalty, giving the berated South an opportunity to snicker.

Charles was sentenced to death in October 1983 for killing a young couple and robbing them. He eventually gave up his appeals, allowing the state to speed his way to execution by lethal injection.

Nearly half of his 50 years on Earth were spent in prisons. He had three previous convictions for burglary and larceny. He received 10-20 years in 1969 for attempted murder — he attacked his girlfriend — but was paroled in 1977. Another robbery put him in jail again until 1981, and he was on parole until 1982.

Then on June 18, 1983, Charles made the biggest mistake of his life. He was at Silver Creek, near his hometown of Mascoutah, Illinois, when he came across Kevin Paule and Sharon Winkler, who were enjoying a day of fishing. The three struck up a conversation — then Charles decided to rob them.

He robbed Kevin and Sharon of all the money they had — $40. Brandishing a handgun, he used duct tape to tie them to a nearby tree. It might have ended there, with Charles leaving with the $40, the fishing tackle and Sharon's car. But Kevin yelled out that he recognized Charles and that he "can't get away with this." Charles responded with two pistol shots, one through Kevin's head and the other through Sharon's. Kevin was right, however. Charles didn't get away with it.

A few years later, Charles decided to let Illinois' political genies grant him his death wish, and he dropped his appeals. Despite the pleas of attorneys and various abolitionist groups, the courts stepped out of the way and opened the execution chamber doors.

Chuck Sheidel, whom I was on my way to see this morning, was one of the lawyers who wanted Charles to change his mind.

He was also Charles' friend, one of the only people on Earth with that distinction.

Chuck had a different view of Charles, as might be expected. He didn't deny his client's guilt, to which Charles himself readily admitted. Chuck did deny the validity of the legal process, however, and questioned whether Charles Walker was truly the pathological killer and threat to society he was made out to be.

Our conversation would be Chuck's first with a journalist since the execution. I popped a fresh set of batteries into my tape recorder, packed up my things and opened the door to brave the cold Springfield morning, my jacket zipped to the top and the collar tucked around my ears.

My hotel was only a few blocks from the Illinois Capital Collateral Office, Chuck Sheidel's home away from home. After waiting for what seemed like half an hour, I finally was waved into an office by a gregarious secretary who babbled along as if I were the first human she had spoken to in weeks.

Chuck remained behind his relatively bare wooden desk when I walked in, though he extended a hearty handshake and smile. Even sitting down his tall, lanky frame was apparent. As it turned out, he was an avid basketball fan and player, but he admitted his legal briefs looked much better than his jump shot.

Chuck talked like a lawyer, which as far as I could tell was his only major weakness. But he was passionate, that was for sure — about Charles Walker; about the law; and especially about the inequity of the death penalty.

Chuck's office, much like Larry Spaulding's office in Florida, is the clearinghouse for all of Illinois' Death Row appeals. At first, Chuck liked his job.

"I thought the death penalty would be exciting and challenging," he said. "But it's going to be a lot more depressing in the years to come than it has been in the '80s."

Opposition to the death penalty among Illinois jurists had been eroding for years, Chuck said, to the point where Charles' execution finally was made possible. The Illinois law actually was struck down in 1979 by a trial court, but the State Supreme Court reversed the decision a year later. Although serious questions still persisted, the high court eventually began affirming death cases.

"The court was upset that the United States Supreme Court didn't take the case out of its hands and solve the (Constitutionality) problem for them," Chuck said. "Appeals kept coming to them, and I think after a while, they became jaded because they were hearing us make the same arguments. They were holding death penalty cases to a stricter standard of procedural default than other cases.

"There's a part of me that hopes that because there has been an execution...the reality of the death penalty has an effect on the way in which they look at cases. Maybe they will take the cases more seriously, but it's impossible to say for sure. There is so much subjectivity with the death penalty, it's not a black-and-white kind of thing. When you get to the question of does some person need to die, that goes beyond a simple finding of reasonable doubt.

"One of the most frustrating things is that the State Supreme Court has the power to say the death penalty is not appropriate in a particular case, even if it fits the guidelines. They are making the same sort of emotional, moral decision a jury makes." Chuck admitted that some of the court's callousness has spread to him, too.

"It's hard not to become somewhat callous about this whole thing after a while, in terms of how much emotion you can summon up for a particular case," he said. "Your first death penalty case is a cause, it's a personal, emotional kind of thing. But 50 cases, that's a job. You simply can't be emotionally attached to 50 clients."

Charles, however, was one client to which Chuck was emotionally attached. Chuck was appointed in 1984 to handle Charles' appeals — but in 1985, Charles asked that his appeals be dropped. No amount of pleading could persuade him to change his mind. Nevertheless, Chuck stayed in touch, up to the final weeks. He wasn't ashamed to call Charles his friend.

"He made an afghan for me, and a blanket for my baby when it was born," Chuck said. "I grew very attached to him. He was personable and bright, liked to talk about baseball and his nieces and nephews, liked to give you advice about things. He didn't like law or talking much about the case. He had spent most of his life in prison, and he simply didn't want to spend the rest of it there. He made it pretty hard to argue with. Down deep, I really didn't think he was ever going to change his mind."

Most upsetting to Chuck is the feeling that Charles might have been able to win if he had continued his appeals. When Charles was on trial, the least sentence he could have received from the jury was life in prison without parole. Yet court transcripts show that the state prosecutor, perhaps unaware of the new state law allowing life without parole, told the jury that the minimum sentence Charles could receive was 20 years. If you don't give him death, the prosecutor said, Charles could be free to walk the streets.

Chuck raised the issue on appeal. But because Charles' defense attorney failed to correct the prosecutor at trial, the appeals court ruled that it was procedural default, not a miscarriage of justice. In other words, sure, the defense attorney made a mistake, but he had his chance — tough luck, Charles.

"The defense attorney didn't know the law, either," Chuck said angrily. "Neither did the judge. Had Charles decided to go on, that issue might have won in federal court.

"There is a big disparity in the idea that if we have the death penalty, it will be reasonably obtained. There are aspects of arbitrariness that always exist. The whole procedural default thing is outrageous."

Chuck tried everything he could to get Charles to fight. One time, Chuck got one of his former clients — one of Charles' friends on Death Row whom Chuck managed to get off on appeal — to write a letter to Charles asking him to change his mind. Charles wrote back:

"You have seen many lay in these cages and grow old, enduring the suffering and misery, the loneliness, without proper medical treat-

ment, the petty bullshit, the static of all these damn fools and idiots. So it's senseless to lay in one of these cages enduring all that when the end result is still the same — death. As we both know, I'll never see the streets again...that's just the way the cookie crumbles."

Part of Charles' reason for dying, Chuck said, was a desire to show his family that he was ashamed of what he had done to them. Chuck said Charles' family had mixed feelings about his death.

"Some were more concerned about it than others," he said. "One of his sisters spent a lot of time trying to talk him out of it, but his mom wasn't willing to join in any of the lawsuits to keep him from execution. His brother opposed anyone trying to stop the execution."

Chuck said the last time he saw Charles was two weeks before the execution.

"We talked about the St. Louis Cardinals, the same old stuff," he said. "I talked to him by phone a week before, and sent him a letter thanking him for the stuff he made for us. I went to the execution and held a candle outside, but I didn't go inside. I kind of wish I could have said good-bye.

"Charles was an alcoholic, and was intoxicated at the time of the crime. But if you met him, you would find it hard to reconcile the murder with Charles. He was a model prisoner, and got along well with the guards.

"I miss him," Chuck said after a long pause. "I keep thinking that he'll call and talk about basketball or something."

Chuck kept second-guessing his representation of Charles until the time of execution. He seemed unable — or unwilling — to convince himself that he had done the best he could.

"The night of the execution...this huge event was happening," he said. "People were directing traffic for parking, like it was the state fair, and I kept thinking that this enormous thing is something that wouldn't be happening if we had done something different. It was my responsibility that the case wasn't handled better.

"But I was just one of the masses milling around the prison," he said. "I felt like Waldo, just one of this huge mob of people —

but I knew the guy. I worked on his case, and I felt we could have prevented the whole thing."

Compounding Chuck's frustration was the carnival atmosphere surrounding the execution. Some were singing "na na na na, hey Walker, good-bye." The whole sight made him angry, and made him wonder whether people really have the capacity to change.

"What is it that makes people pro or anti something like this?" he said. "One of the things that has happened to me in this job is that I'm less energized about arguing the morality of this thing, and most of that is the futility that you're not going to change people's minds.

"I'm more concerned about trying to inform people," Chuck said. "There is still this fear that these guys are going to get released, and that is simply not true.

"It's hard for me to imagine 1,000 executions, but there is nothing to stop that except abolition. I guess there is every reason to think there are going to be large numbers of executions all over the country in this decade, though I have trouble envisioning a country where it is such a routine thing.

"The message it sends is that this is a mean world, and if you fuck up, you're going to get it," he said, relaxing a bit in his chair. "We're tired of sob stories, and we're tired of the amount of crime. But I can't imagine that anyone is going to feel safer. My perspective on deterrence is based on clients that we have had, and deterrence isn't really a big factor.

"But people are affected by emotions more than facts and figures. In the big picture, what's going on here is really a simplistic, superficial approach to crime. The people we see are almost universally deprived, abused, uneducated, afflicted by alcoholism and drugs. The idea that if we execute a bunch of people that those problems still won't create murderers is ridiculous.

"The greatest harm from the death penalty and people in general is the thought that we're doing something about crime, and we're not," he said. "It's troubling to see the amount of public support for that. It's crazy."

At that moment, a young lawyer walked in to ask Chuck a question about a case. Chuck relaxed, obviously relieved to get a break from the interview. It was about time for me to hit the road anyway, so I used the interruption to gather my things and say good-bye.

Chuck thanked me for coming, and for giving him a chance to get some things off his chest.

"I just stopped talking to reporters after a while," Chuck said as he showed me out. "I just didn't feel like talking."

I walked outside into the November chill toward my car, which was parked across the street at the State Capitol. I climbed inside, blasted the heater and the stereo and headed northeast to Chicago. Nothing colder than an Illinois winter — absolutely nothing.

I awoke the next day in a friend's apartment on Chicago's northside. My friend, John, was a reporter for a wire service, and was getting ready to go into work. I, on the other hand, was getting ready for two more interviews and a drive to Columbia, Missouri, for a reunion with my fiancee and a meeting with inmates on Missouri's Death Row.

John and I are political animals, though we had never deeply discussed our personal political views. He is a Republican and I am a Democrat, but that was it. So I was somewhat surprised at dinner the previous night when John and I got into an involved discussion over the death penalty.

Maybe, John said, as in the book *A Clockwork Orange*, prisons are simply unable to reform people. We either can't or don't know how to help them, so our only response, our only way of dealing with it, is to get rid of these people. I pretended I understood what he was saying, though I had a hard time believing that no one can ever be helped, some way, somehow. Capital punishment, even in his world, only cured the symptoms of a society's disease.

On the way to his office, John mentioned that a friend of his, a radio reporter, had been one of the official witnesses at Charles' execution. Although he wasn't sure, John said he might be willing to talk about it. So while John perused the morning newspapers, I put in a call to Mike Doyle, a reporter and anchor at Chicago news station WMAQ.

I got Mike on the phone, and after a bit of coaxing, talked to him about his experience. He said his station was picked in a lottery drawing among news organizations interested in covering the execution, and was optimistic about the experience when his news director asked him to go.

"I said, 'Sure, why not?' I had a bit of apprehension, and a lot of questions in my mind about seeing someone die. I was still somewhat nervous and apprehensive up to the night it happened."

Mike described the minutes leading to Charles' death.

"I went into a briefing room with about 10 other reporters," he said. "We talked about Walker and his case, and shared our nervous feelings. We then walked across a huge courtyard, which was surrounded by cellblocks. It was real eerie. It was dark, there was a full moon, and the air had a hollow sound. We heard inmates yelling at us, but we couldn't see them. They yelled, 'Murderers! Go home and tell your children!' It was quite unsettling.

"Then we went into the witness room. In front of us was a window with vertical blinds, closed, and we heard a nervous coughing on the other side of the window. At midnight, they pulled open the blinds, and we were face to face with Walker. He turned and looked at us. He was three feet in front of us. It made my heart jump being so close; I felt uneasy about it. He looked at us, then turned his head upward.

"He was on a gurney and had an I.V. bottle hooked up to his arm. At exactly midnight, he took two or three huge breaths, his right arm flicked, his head turned to the right and he stopped breathing. He was covered with a blanket up to his neck. He stayed there for 10 to 15 minutes before he officially was pronounced dead, and we just looked at him on the gurney.

"During that time, I was thinking about how clinical it was, how fast and apparently painless. It looked like an easy way out for someone who wanted to die. It was an easy escape from incarceration. It seemed to make death palatable."

Witnessing Walker's execution, Mike said, changed his mind about capital punishment.

"I've never been passionate about the death penalty," he said. "As a reporter, when I covered stories about some of these horrible crimes, I've thought, 'I really hope they execute this guy, I hope they fry him.' But after seeing it...it seemed that the death penalty was too easy a way to go.

"I think it would be a more appropriate punishment to let them rot in jail the rest of their lives," Mike said. "I probably would witness an execution again if I was assigned to it and had to go, but I have no real desire to do it again.

"I thought about the execution when I was driving back to Chicago, at about 2:30 a.m. on a lonely highway. I thought that I would never do it again. If it was an electric chair rather than lethal injection, I might have balked at it the first time. I would not have wanted to see that. I would have had a lot of nightmares."

Mike had to get back to work, so I quickly thanked him and walked over to John's desk to say good-bye. John gave me directions on how to get to my next appointment, which wasn't too difficult since I was just going across the street.

My appointment was with one of Illinois' most experienced death penalty scholars. His name is Seymour Simon: grandfather, attorney-at-law, and former justice on the Illinois State Supreme Court. I called Seymour a lawyer, and indeed that's what it says on his business card. But throughout much of our interview, he spent the bulk of his time talking to relatives and visiting with old friends — old in every sense; as I arrived, I passed by Seymour's previous guest, a man in his mid-80s whom Simon met when they were in high school together.

Seymour himself is the kind of character who must stay active if only for the sake of staying active. His office is littered with numerous awards and acclamations, and pictures from his days on his state's high court.

Seymour served on the Illinois Supreme Court from 1980 to 1987, forgoing his full 10-year term because, as he put it, he grew tired of driving to Springfield for 16 weeks out of each year to hold sessions. During that time, however, he estimates he must have heard more than 90 death penalty cases.

I related my talk with Chuck to Seymour, and he agreed that Charles had valid grounds for a successful appeal.

"Walker's initial death sentence hearing was full of victim impact testimony," Seymour said. "That kind of testimony should have no place in a death hearing. The result is, well, if you kill a bum, a wino, a drug addict, then you shouldn't get the death penalty. But if you kill an upright person, a decent person, a good citizen, then you should get it. Well, that is no reason to have a death penalty.

"I dissented from Walker when I was on the court, because I felt it was state-sponsored suicide," Seymour said. "Who is he to get his will? He was a murderer. The public had no obligation to accede to his wishes." Seymour said he was surprised, and somewhat disheartened, that the Charles Walker execution was allowed to proceed.

"It was bad to have a first execution of someone who wasn't resisting execution," Seymour said between phone calls. "It didn't sit right. It made me a participant in the execution of the person who wanted to get it.

"We were accommodating him. We should have said, 'If you think it's a terrible thing in your life to stay behind bars, then you should get that punishment.' It's a punishment to be locked up in jail. Besides, it costs more to execute them than it does to keep them in jail."

Although as a member of the court, Seymour was sworn to uphold his state's laws, including capital punishment, he said that he has always opposed executions because, in the end, they don't make things better.

"It's useless, it doesn't do any good," Seymour said. "It cannot be imposed in any other way but a chancy manner. The public is mad about crime and they want to do something about it, they want retribution. But when people realize how chancy the imposition of the death penalty is, people are going to start getting concerned about it. Once you have the death penalty, it doesn't stop there. Where do you draw the line? All murder is a heinous crime, but there are degrees of offensiveness.

"I think public opinion can be changed, and over time it will. The more executions that occur, the more the public will be repulsed by the death sentences. We had the Walker execution last week, and we still have more murders in Chicago."

Seymour had to cut our interview short because he had a luncheon appointment. We said good-bye and, again, I found myself outside braving that Illinois chill.

One more interview to go, and then on to Missouri. After that, home. First, though, I had to find Davis Street in Evanston, the offices of Andrea D. Lyon, Attorney At Law.

Professionally, Lyon is a mirror image of Alabama prosecutor Jimmy Fry. A defense trial lawyer who represents capital defendants, Andrea has never lost a client to Death Row — 40 death cases, 16 penalty trials, and no one on Death Row. That's not lucky, that's good. Damn good.

I first learned about Andrea Lyon from "60 Minutes". The weekly newsmagazine did a story about a young man named Steve Shores who happened to be in the wrong place at the wrong time. Steve witnessed two local gang members gun down a security guard, and was threatened by the gang to keep his mouth shut, or else the same fate would meet his family.

Steve, who lived in the Chicago housing projects, kept his mouth shut even when the gang members fingered him for the murder. Steve was convicted and sent to prison. His attorney was Andrea Lyon.

"He thought because he wasn't guilty that he wouldn't be found guilty," Andrea said in the "60 Minutes" interview. "He believed that the system would figure out what was true and that he could still protect himself and his family by remaining silent."

He was wrong. When Steve finally decided to tell the real story, his 31-year-old sister was murdered, dropped from a 12th-floor window.

I walked up the two flights of stairs to Andrea's comfortably messy office, where she was just finishing a conversation with Steve Shores' mother. Andrea, a tall, stocky woman with jet black hair, was telling Mrs. Shores that her son was being moved to a different prison because of death threats he had received from gang members inside. All in a day's work for Illinois' hardest working defense attorney.

Andrea, sitting behind a desk cluttered with books and papers, said hard work is why she has been so successful at keeping her clients as far from Death Row as possible.

"Some of it is luck and my level of advocacy, but a lot of it has to do with preparation," Andrea said. "It's about getting ready to do the penalty phase before the trial phase begins. I'm not assuming I'm gonna lose, I'm just getting ready. I don't think you can prepare every possible thing, but you certainly can do a good job.

"I don't really want to deal with the death penalty," she said. "It's scary, it's always emotional. No one on the jury ever votes with their heads, they vote with their hearts. What I do is try to take out the lack of humanity in a courtroom, the cold-hearted killing atmosphere, and get back to normalcy. That way somebody can make a decision without ignoring their heart, and without responding only to the one emotion that the prosecution enjoys and engenders — and that's fear. Fear is what puts people on Death Row."

Andrea doesn't try to hide her passionate dislike for her courtroom adversaries.

"I have never tried a case where the prosecution didn't cheat," she said. "They just do. They don't get ahead unless they look tough, mean, cold, and get convictions. Do you think the

United States Supreme Court gives a shit about defendants? They don't. It's counter-intuitive to presume innocence."

Another key to Andrea's success is her ability to put question marks into jurors' heads. Where there is a defendant, she believes, there is always some degree of doubt.

"I've won a lot of my cases in the death hearing because I put a lot of doubt about guilt into the trial phase," Andrea said. "The most important thing you have to think about is what color is everybody. Racism is everywhere, and Chicago is one of the most divisive places in the world. It's the single most important thing: what color is the victim, and what color is the client."

For years, Andrea worked in the Chicago Public Defender's Office. She was the only woman on the department's homicide task force, and later became its head. All along, Andrea opposed capital punishment. Some things, she said, belong to God — death is one of them.

"I don't think there is any way to factor out the things that are factored into the death penalty," she said. "How do you factor out racism, publicity, election year? You can't. There is going to be human error, and biases and prejudices that are going to affect the outcome.

"The death penalty is not going to stop until we kill several demonstrably innocent people — and we will. America is spoiled rotten and doesn't understand what we've got here, and doesn't understand what we're giving up by embracing barbaric, simple answers to complex questions. The death penalty costs a lot of money, it doesn't protect anyone, and it increases our own violence. We won't get upset until someone — preferably someone white — dies.

"We're a schizophrenic society," Andrea said, sipping coffee from a styrofoam cup. "We condemn Ted Bundy, but admire Jesse James. People want Ted Bundy killed so they can deny their violent selves, but the truth is, we all have a killer in us. Under one circumstance or another, we all could do it."

Andrea said there is only one guarantee that she will never lose a death penalty case — that she never try another one. She is terrified of losing, though she admits that one day it inevitably is going to happen.

"The day I'm no longer terrified is the day I quit, because that means I no longer care," she said. "We can teach people to see things in a different way if we do the work. In this business you think about God, about how people suffer, so many things. But it just makes me appreciate life more. And I think that, like most of us, I know that I'll die sometime, though I really don't believe it. But when I do, there will be some things that I've done in this world that have been worth doing.

"There are 16 people who got to live because of me, and maybe there will be a few more. And that's pretty good, y'know?"

We had been talking for some time, and already the sun was beginning its descent. That meant more cold, so I was anxious to get back to my car and my heater, and begin the drive to Missouri.

I had been on the road now for nearly a month, and frankly, I was looking forward to seeing my fiancee and getting a few days to recharge my batteries. A few days of not having to live out of motel rooms; a few days of not getting lost and eating food that has been fried three times too many; a few days free from the constant talk of death.

A few days of life, that's what I wanted. A few days to remind myself that there is a world other than the one where the guilty — and sometimes the innocent — go to jail, where fear is king and hate his ever-present companion.

Unfortunately, a few days was all I was going to get. Soon it would be time for me to revisit the small, one-time mining town of Potosi, home to friendly people, high unemployment and Death Row. It was Potosi, when I was still in college, where I met inmate Gerald Smith.

Like Charles Walker, Gerald Smith also gave up his appeals and was executed. He was the first Death Row inmate I ever met, and I never forgot him. So now I was going to go back to Potosi, to see how the town had changed, if at all, and to meet some of the inmates Gerald Smith left behind — a bittersweet reunion at best. I wondered, as my car flew past the Gateway Arch and the lights of Downtown St. Louis, whether the inmates I talked to this time would be the next to die — like Gerald Smith and Charles Walker; like John Evans, Ray Clark and all the rest.

Some things never seem to change. We can't change the the sun, moon or stars. We can't stop the IRS, the *National Enquirer* or the fact that people are going to kill each other. If we could do that, then we could cure cancer and end world hunger, too.

If we could do that, maybe then we could control the weather. Maybe, then, it wouldn't be so cold.

CHAPTER 11

KILLING TIME

"Most people here never thought about execution. For years and years...we had spent years, killing time, fooling around down here, when in reality we were like lambs being led to slaughter."

— A.J. Bannister, Missouri Death Row inmate

"If it wasn't such a high cost then I would be for the death penalty. But to keep a person for a lifetime is like $375,000, while to put him to death is a million and a half. Everybody is entitled to appeals, and cops do lie. At times, some people are put away who shouldn't be."

— Roger Bildeback, president of the Potosi Chamber of Commerce

"A National Food Center store in St. Louis was held up and robbed, seven people were shot and five died. Two guys went to trial, and they were given life sentences. I mean, my God, we don't have anybody on Death Row who has killed five people."

— Carolyn Atkins, Lincoln University criminology professor

It happened innocently enough. I walked into the *Columbia Missourian* newsroom one day in 1988 to get my mail, and one of my college professors pulled me aside and asked if I had some time to do a story for the weekend edition. Without asking what the story was about, I said yes, not wanting to miss an opportunity to make my teacher happy.

The story was about Gerald Smith, who was set to die in Missouri's gas chamber in a matter of weeks. His plight soon filled my waking hours, as I poured through reams of clips and court documents that took me into the background of a confessed murderer.

Smith, one of Missouri's most brutal killers, stood a good chance of becoming the first person executed in the state in 23 years. A good chance because of one unusual factor: like Charles Walker, he wanted to die. He had many appeals left, opportunity upon opportunity to live a little longer. But that didn't matter. The killer wanted to die, and the state was more than willing to oblige.

Even those vehemently opposed to the death penalty admitted that Smith's crimes deserved to be called brutal. Upset because he thought his ex-girlfriend, Karen Roberts, had given him a venereal disease, Smith beat the 20-year-old woman to death on a dark St. Louis street one night in 1980. He chased her for blocks, across a set of railroad tracks, before finally crushing her skull with an 8-pound iron bar. He left her body to God and walked home.

He confessed several days later and was charged with first-degree murder. His confession was short, not all that sweet, and very memorable: "I killed the bitch," he said.

I'll never forget the day I went to interview Smith in Potosi. We met in a dimly lit room with one wooden table and two wooden chairs. In a corner, a stout female prison guard puffed nervously on a cigarette. There was no sound except for her breath and my scribbling, trying to prepare for an interview I already had conducted in my head a thousand times.

Suddenly, the silence was broken by two sets of footsteps coming from behind the door. I heard the jingle of keys and saw the thick, steel barrier open to reveal a young, unsmiling guard and a 31-year-old man, shackled by the legs and arms.

He was Caucasian, thin, sporting a mustache. He looked toward the floor, never smiling or showing any sign of emotion.

His face was cold, so cold that I had a sudden image of his tears, if he could cry, freezing before they could roll down his cheeks.

Our talk was brief; Smith didn't have much he wanted to say, and I didn't have much leverage for getting him to talk. I couldn't "make" Gerald Smith tell me something he didn't want to tell me, because that was one right he still controlled. I could ask my questions, but neither I nor the prison could dictate his will to answer them.

After 10 minutes, Smith got up and left. His execution date was postponed for months, though my subsequent attempts to talk to Smith failed. Finally, in early 1990, Smith got his wish — the killer who wanted to die was put to death by lethal injection.

The road to Potosi winds through some of the most beautiful countryside in the United States, but on this morning it was dark and cold and looked like it might rain — or worse, snow. That prospect didn't weigh on me too heavily at that point, though. I had just spent several wonderful days with Christine, and slept on a mattress that wasn't stuffed at the local rock quarry. Soon, I would be heading back home, my mission accomplished. I was actually starting to look forward to hunting for a job and returning to something that resembled a normal life.

So the thought of an icy, dangerous drive didn't really bother me; the men I was about to visit on Missouri's Death Row would probably give anything for that chance.

Before going to Potosi, however, I first made a stop in Jefferson City, the state Capital. It was on the way along U.S. 63 South, and I wanted to stop and talk to Carolyn Atkins. Carolyn, a stout black woman with thin strands of curly hair, is a criminology professor at Lincoln University in Jefferson City. I couldn't spend much time with her, but I at least wanted to shoot the breeze for a while.

Lincoln University is on the second highest hill in Jefferson City. It's just a stone's throw from the Capitol building and the banks of the mighty Missouri River, and has rolling green grounds that resemble ski slopes in the wintertime.

I found Carolyn in her cubbyhole office, grading papers and getting ready for final exams. She seemed anxious for a break, even if that break meant discussing capital punishment. Carolyn is strongly opposed to the death penalty. The inequity of the punishment, she said, is the most troublesome factor.

"A National Food Center store in St. Louis was held up and robbed, seven people were shot and five died," she said, filling me in on a recent case. "Two guys went to trial, and they were given life sentences. I mean, my God, we don't have anybody on Death Row who has killed five people.

"Another example: there was a fellow who was a member of The Order, a neo-Nazi group, who lived in southern Missouri. He was driving his van on Interstate 44 when he was stopped by two highway patrolmen. The driver climbed out of his van and shot both officers. He got a change of venue to Columbia, which is a fairly cosmopolitan area for Missouri, and got a life sentence.

"Now there was another fella who was arrested, handcuffed and put in a highway patrolman's car," Carolyn said. "Somehow he got the officer's gun and killed him. They changed the venue to a little town in northeast Missouri, where they never had a murder and never had a black. He got the death penalty. So, it's obvious that we're still doing this in an inequitable way."

We talked for a while about her work, politics and the state of my former home state. I told her that I was headed to Potosi, which made her eyes light up since she had made many trips there herself for her doctoral research.

Carolyn is one of those people whose opposition to capital punishment is so clear, so simple and to the point, that it makes you wonder how anyone could possibly be in favor of it. We agreed that while common sense dictates abolition, sense is something all too uncommon in the national death penalty debate.

"The death penalty is a superfluous procedure," Carolyn said. "It's more expensive than it's worth. But how do you change attitudes when we have more crime now than we've ever had? Something we're doing is not right. No one ever stops and thinks that maybe we should stop and look at it. We have an entrenched mentality, and until we get off that point, we're not going anywhere.

"The public has never understood that their house is not safe until everybody is safe," she said. "It's not 'just as long as it doesn't happen in my neighborhood'."

Carolyn wished me well on my trip, and soon I was on my way, first going east on State Route 68 and then taking route 8 into Potosi. Along the way is a string of small towns, such as St. James and Steelville. Two lanes are as big as the highways get around here, and cows still wander through farm fields. Once in a while, though, the occasional satellite dish pops up and spoils the Rockwellian flavor of it all. Before Death Row, Potosi's greatest claim to fame was being named the population center of the United States in 1976. A marker on the edge of town pays tribute to that fact.

I stopped downtown for lunch and a quick visit to Roger Bildeback, president of the Potosi Chamber of Commerce, whom I'd interviewed the last time I was in Potosi.

All along Main Street there were holiday wreaths on trees and light poles to help usher in the season. Ma & Pa's Restaurant was still here, though there was a new shopping center and gas station. There also was a Kentucky Fried Chicken outlet and a Wal-Mart, which probably could hold all of the town's residents at one time.

The prison apparently did bring some financial benefit. You've got to feed all those visiting sheriff's deputies, and have places for the prison personnel and their families to shop. Life does go on.

The Potosi Correctional Center is technically in Mineral Point, just outside the Potosi city limits. But since Mineral Point actually has fewer people than Potosi, it lost the right to be the prison's namesake. The prison is on Highway O, about a half-mile from downtown Potosi. The first sight you get of the facility is a lone guard tower peaking over the terrain. A little closer, you can see a light beige Chevy stationwagon patrolling the bridge. The security here seems relatively unobtrusive, but it's actually air tight — let me explain.

Anyone who has ever visited a prison before knows that you must pass through a metal detector before entering the cell area. These detectors are a hell of a lot more sensitive than the airport variety, and can drive you nuts. After I checked in with the guard at the visitor's desk, I walked over to the metal detector with my passes to see Doyle Williams and A.J. Bannister, two inmates who agreed to my interview request. In front of me was a young man, barely in his 30's, carrying an overstuffed leather briefcase. Everything about him said Lawyer.

But Joe Law School couldn't get past the metal detector. He was practically naked by the time the guard figured out it was his shoelace rings that were causing all the commotion. He sheepishly apologized and muttered that he had never been to a prison before.

It didn't take a Harvard Law graduate to figure out that this guy was as inexperienced as they come. After a few seconds of small talk, I learned that he was going to see a client — a man on Death Row. As I suspected, it was his first death case. I felt almost as sorry for the lawyer as for his client.

A friendly female guard led me through the maze of ultra-violet hand stamp checkpoints and computerized doorways, until finally we reached the prison interview area. There were rows of long, gray tables surrounded by turquoise green chairs. Everything looked very clean, very sterile and neat. An automatic sign on the wall was blinking, "Have a nice day."

Vending machines offered feasts of chips, candy, soda and coffee; the cigarette machine, obviously the most popular, was half-empty. At the far end of the room, near a row of numbered telephone interview stalls, a family was visiting with a relative at one of the tables, enjoying a bag of microwave popcorn and the video game "Ms. Pac-Man".

After about 10 minutes, a short, balding man with glasses and a beard came bounding out of a doorway. It was Doyle

Williams, and although we had only talked by phone, he acted as if we had known each other for years.

"How about buying us a Pepsi," Doyle asked, in a voice the speed of light. Somewhat embarrassed and surprised, I confessed that I didn't have any money with me. He appeared rather dejected, and wondered aloud why I would come to see an inmate and not bring any money for the vending machines. The answer was because the inmate would ask me to spend it, but I kept my reasons to myself, and changed the topic.

Doyle, I quickly learned, was raised in North Carolina, and came to Missouri in his teens. In 1980, at age 33, he was convicted in the killing of 28-year-old Kerry Brummett of Jefferson City. Kerry, who knew that Doyle had burglarized a doctor's office, was handcuffed when he ran into the Missouri River and drowned, apparently in an attempt to flee Doyle, who had beaten him with a pistol.

The state contends that Doyle pushed Kerry into the river; Doyle said he tried to save Kerry, who according to Doyle jumped in the river. But Doyle doesn't deny he's responsible for a man's death.

"Once I was found guilty of capital murder, I knew I was better off with a death sentence than with life in prison without parole," said Doyle, who fancies himself as somewhat of a legal expert, and was described by prison officials as the most litigious of all Death Row inmates. "I had better odds of getting a reversal with a death sentence."

Nine years later, Doyle did get that reversal. A three-judge panel of the 8th U.S. Circuit Court of Appeals said the jurors who convicted him should have been allowed to consider a first-degree murder charge, as other juries had been allowed in similar cases.

The victory, however, was short-lived. The ruling was appealed to the full Circuit Court, and Doyle's death penalty conviction was upheld. Three months after our conversation, Doyle came within just a few hours of being executed by lethal injection, saved only by a last-minute court order.

"Since they took my reversal away, I've thought about the death penalty more," Doyle said, unaware of the situation he would face in about 90 days. "You can't prepare for it, you can only experience it when it occurs. I'd like to know what I'd do, but I don't.

"Every soldier knows that when he goes onto a battlefield, he could be killed, but he doesn't think it could be him," he said. "Well, we're on Death Row. We know when we will be executed. But what good would it be to sit around and whine about it? It doesn't do any good at all."

The more Doyle tried to be aloof about the whole execution process, the more I believed he was hiding his fear. This was a man who put on a mask for his fellow inmates and visitors, an appearance of strength and courage.

But he was faking it. I knew it, and I'm sure he did, too. While calling for swift, public executions, he also explained why the death penalty was wrong. He wanted me to believe that his sentence didn't matter, but it wasn't working. Unfortunately, neither were my attempts to bypass his bullet train delivery and get to his emotions. So I listened, first to the Doyle Williams who supports the death penalty:

"Everyone on Death Row who is guilty believes in capital punishment," he said. "They believe it's right to take a person's life. If you ask the inmates what they would do if their sister was raped, they'd say, 'I'd kill the SOB.'

"If you want to make the death penalty a deterrent, then let's have executions on the Fourth of July under the Arch. When you do it 150 miles away, at night, no one will believe it's wrong. Out of sight, out of mind. I think the death penalty would be popular if you executed people 10 days after the trial."

Then I heard the anti-death penalty Doyle Williams:

"I don't think the state should kill," he said with the same fervor. "It's like the speed limit. It applies to everyone, it's not 75 mph just for the rich. The death penalty is not black and white, it's arbitrary. I could have plead guilty to 30 years, but I threw the dice. There are 80 people here on Death Row, but there are 300 others here convicted of the same crimes, and they didn't get the death penalty."

And, perhaps, the real Doyle Williams:

"I don't want to die," he said, his volume lowering for the first time in nearly 45 minutes. "I'm not looking forward to going to sleep and not waking up. Human nature is to want to live.

"If I knew I had no other way out except death, I would commit suicide. I would buy a couple hundred dollars worth of barbiturates and end it right there.

"I've tried to study and understand the law, and the most fascinating thing is not knowing what will happen with the law," said Doyle, who was being motioned by a nearby guard that it was almost time to leave. "Life in prison without parole is more severe in lots of ways...to sit here for the rest of your life and not get out.

"If I got out, I would like to spend time with my family," he said, turning away from the table. "Then I would like to pass the bar and practice law." Doyle smiled broadly. "I think I'd be pretty good," he said.

We shook hands, and I promised to bring some change on my next visit. But unless he slowed the speed of his chatter, I told him, it would have to be caffeine free. Doyle had to leave because it was time for the inmates to eat supper. Because of that, I had to wait about 20 more minutes before my second interview, Alan "A.J." Bannister, would be able to join me.

While I waited, I couldn't help noticing a group of three people — apparently an inmate and his family — sitting at one of the nearby tables. Every five minutes or so, one of them would get up and go to one of the vending machines. They would buy popcorn, candy, soda, whatever was available. And they didn't really talk, they just sat and ate and wondered what to purchase next.

The vending machines were to them the greatest luxury in the world. It was freedom, the ability to eat what you want, when you want it. The machine made them more human. In prison, you try to grab as much freedom as you can, no matter how insignificant it may seem.

While I mulled that over, I heard the door open again and in walked A.J., still carrying his dinner tray. He appeared young for 31, with shoulder-length brown hair and rose-colored, John Lennon style glasses. On the menu for today's supper, by the way, looked to be some sort of meat stew, two pieces of white bread and cole slaw.

Those who knew him said A.J. was articulate and gentle, and indeed, in just the few words we exchanged in greeting, I could tell that this was no Doyle Williams. Instead of being hyper and at times unintelligible, A.J. spoke with an unmistakable air of sophistication.

He was raised in Central Illinois, the oldest of six children. One of A.J.'s brothers served in the Persian Gulf War. A.J. described his background as middle-class, a kid with lots of freedom because his parents were always too busy to watch after him. From 1975 to 1983, his arrest record included unlawful use of weapons, assault, rape, possession of marijuana, and obstruction of justice. On paper, at least, he was no Eagle Scout.

His first brush with trouble was at age 11, when he threw a rock through a train window. At age 17, A.J.'s friend looted a parking lot, and because he didn't want his friend to get in all that trouble alone, A.J. took the blame with him and served nine months in the Illinois State Penitentiary.

"I left prison with the wrong attitude," said A.J., who picked up some bad habits from older cons who befriended him. "I got caught up in a burglary just six months after my release. I knew I was going to get a parole violation anyway, so I took the brunt of the blame. I got two-to-six years, and the other guys got 90 days on work release."

A.J. spent another 18 months in prison, but when he got out, it was the same story: he hadn't learned a thing.

"I got a job with the Chillicothe (Mo.) Street Department, but I got laid off without much notice," he said. "Then I got a job with Allied Welder through my dad. But I quit that job, and then made really no effort to get another one. I took a gas station job for giggles; I used to give away free gas.

"I started drinking and doing drugs. I always had a good relationship with my family, but they secretly wished that I would change, and realized that I had to do it on my own."

A.J. got involved in a statutory rape, and after weighing whether he should turn himself in, opted to go to Texas. He went back to Illinois after a while, but still made no serious attempt to get a job and straighten out his life.

"I then robbed a 7-11 at gunpoint and robbed a prostitute, all in one night," A.J. said. "I got what was supposed to be 15 years, but I made a deal with the record keeper, and only got put down for 2 and a half years. I always had a nagging feeling that someone would review the paperwork, but no one did."

When A.J. got out, he finally got some work — in drug trafficking. Eventually, his dealings led to Phoenix, and the beginning of the end. One night, outside a night club, A.J. was stabbed repeatedly by a group of three men who apparently thought that A.J. had run off with their cocaine. A.J. said he had given the coke to a mutual friend to return it, but the friend took a while to do it, and in the meantime A.J. was blamed for taking off with the merchandise. A.J. thought he had straightened it out, but apparently the damage already had been done, and the word was out that A.J. couldn't be trusted. He was stabbed six times in the back. They left him for dead, but somehow A.J. survived the attack and made it back to Illinois.

A.J. got the name of the Missouri drug supplier whom he believed had tried to get him killed. He was determined to get revenge.

"I made it clear that I was gonna come down here and hurt this guy — cut him, make him feel what I felt. Then a friend gave me a .22-caliber pistol to do the job, and I took it. I came here and found where the guy lived," he said. "But it didn't seem right; the guy didn't seem like a coke dealer.

"I never actually hurt anyone in the past, and I was having second thoughts about shooting him. I thought I could hit him with a baseball bat, so he would bleed to death. Then I thought I could threaten him and not shoot at all.

"I went to the door and knocked," A.J. continued. "He answered, and I froze up. I said, 'I'm from Illinois, and I want to know why.' Then he grabbed me, and I tried to hit him with the gun. The biggest question in my life is did my thumb flick the trigger, or was it his forearm? His grip lessened, and he had a deadpan expression. He then turned and got back into his trailer.

A.J. said it was difficult to express how he felt when he learned the man had died.

"There was something really sobering about killing a man," he said. "But there was a sense of relief, because I knew he was coming after me." That sense of relief disappeared when A.J. learned he had killed the wrong man. A.J. had killed Darrell Ruestman, who was no drug dealer.

The official story is that A.J. was paid $4,000 by the estranged husband of Ruestman's girlfriend — the husband had a history of paying people to assault Ruestman. At the tender age of 23, A.J. had been labeled a "contract killer" by the state. A.J. said it was a case of mistaken identify, yet he still takes full responsibility for what happened.

"I never had the audacity to say I wasn't there," he said. "I could have, because there were no eyewitnesses. But this was my responsibility. It was my foolishness and anger that took a man's life."

A.J., who got up from the table to take a short cigarette break, had wanted an eye for an eye, and now society wanted the same from him. But instead of revenge, prosecutors used the contract murder theory, most likely because it was easier to get a death penalty conviction that way.

"I'm guilty, but the degree of guilt isn't capital murder," A.J. said after returning from his break. "I didn't point the gun at the man and kill him; I didn't even intend to kill him. If I was really out to kill him, I would have fired five more rounds. I have regrets, and remorse for the victim. I finally got to grow up; it just happened a few years too late."

Unlike his past experiences with prison life, A.J. said some good has come out of the years spent on Death Row. He said it has given him time to reflect on the past, and gain greater respect for things he used to take for granted.

"I wrote a poem for a contest once," he said. "I thought about the things I'm missing: the sound of kids laughing, Thanksgiving dinners. I never paid attention to it before. I wish I could see more kids laughing, perhaps a paternal instinct not realized; the smell of a home cooked meal; birds chirping — little things. Just listening to it, being able to appreciate it. An appreciation for being able to do something for someone, if just to say 'good morning'."

Something else A.J. and the other inmates used to take for granted were stays of executions, but no more. Tiny Mercer changed all that.

Tiny's execution — it happened one year before Gerald Smith — was a reality check for everyone on the Row. For A.J., it was a confirmation of the finality of his surroundings.

"When Tiny was executed, it woke everyone up," A.J. said. "They took a keener interest in their appeals. For years and years...we had spent years, killing time, fooling around down here, when in reality we were like lambs being led to slaughter."

A.J. has a ritual he goes through every night there is an execution somewhere in the United States. He stays awake until the execution is over, and wonders whether someday, someone will do the same for him.

"I would wonder what's going through that man's mind, wonder if a prayer would help," A.J. said. "I don't want to die. But at that point...I don't want to seem weak at the end. Why fight? It's gonna happen anyway.

"When I was stabbed, I thought I was gonna die," he said, leaning toward to me to emphasize his seriousness. "I remember being on the gurney and hearing the orderlies saying, 'I don't know if this one is gonna make it.' There was a feeling of rage, and I wanted to open my eyes and say, 'Hey, I'm not dead yet.' I went on the operating table, and then the lights went out.

"I dreamed about a friend from high school who had died from a suicide. In my dream, I was in a forest. I leaned over a pond, and my high school friend was on the other side of the water. It didn't shock him that I was there, but he shook his head, saying 'no'. Then they hit me with the pacemaker.

"The dream seemed so clear, I was afraid to tell anyone about it. It was a beautiful forest, and it seemed right to be there."

A.J. said all he wants now is a chance to atone for taking a man's life. He can only do that, though, if he's alive.

"Maybe I can't pay back the debt I owe society for taking a life, but I can help others," A.J. said. "I can start paying back for what I've done. I've spent my life taking, and it's important for me to give something back.

"I deserve a sentence for the degree of my guilt, but it's not the death penalty. I've changed, I've been able to look back. I've paid my dues." A.J. suddenly leaned back and cracked a slight smile.

"If I get out, I'm looking for the loosest red head close to here," he said, laughing. "No, I'm just kidding. I'd really like to settle down with a lady friend I've had for about 10 years. I know I can make it into society again," he said, talking as if I were his parole officer. "I'm no longer a wild youth. I have no interest in drugs or getting drunk. I look back at the person I was and think, 'jeez, this guy was a real asshole.'

"Realistically, though, I'm never gonna get out of here," A.J. said, his voice taking a measured, reflective tone. Pointing in the direction of the execution chamber he said, "I'm gonna die of old age or in that little room."

It was time for A.J. to go. My notebook was nearly out of space anyway, and I had another long drive ahead. I didn't fully realize it until just then, but this was the last interview on my trip. My next stop was back home, in California, back to the world of political journalism, or at least I hoped — back to the constricting routine of life in the free world.

I thanked A.J. for his time and promised to keep in touch. "I've got nowhere else to be," he said with a smile. "No hot dates tonight."

It was pitch dark by the time I walked out of the prison. All I could see was the dim glow of barbed wire illuminated by buzzing florescent lights. I knew I was being watched, and I hated it. The parking lot was empty, and it was cold. Maybe it really was going to snow.

It wasn't long before I found my way to Interstate 44, the old Route 66. I could put my car on auto-pilot now. There were no more stops, save for food and coffee. I was going to drive straight through to California. I wasn't at all tired, and besides, it was too cold to sleep, or even to think about what I had experienced the past couple of months.

I did, however, know this: I had moved forward. I did what I had set out to do, and I was a better person for it.

And I was different. California was going to be the same, but I was not. For the first time in my life, I had no idea what the future held, except for my marriage in six months. From now on, I would always be working without a net — I wasn't going to have it any other way.

Arkansas, Oklahoma and Texas. Night surrounded me and I felt that I might float in its grasp forever. I still wasn't tired, just numb from it all. New Mexico and Arizona. I emptied my mind and watched blankly as the miles rolled by, driving automatically, endlessly.

The California border. It was only a matter of hours now before the real world reintroduced itself. There was nothing more for me to do except wait and wonder, this time without fear or self-doubt, what my future would bring.

EPILOGUE

"The problem with these things is that you have more hope than common sense."
—Bill Wiksell, attorney for child killer Greg Smith,
shortly before the announcement of Smith's fate.

I got the call from the court bailiff just past 4 p.m. The jury, after only three days of deliberations, was ready to tell the world whether 21-year-old Gregory Scott Smith would live or die.

I had followed the case for six months, been at all the pre-trial hearings and heard all the testimony. I was in constant conversation with the defense attorneys, and had befriended Greg's mother and sisters. I got to know the prosecutors and Mary Bailly, whose son, Paul...well, Paul is what this was all about.

Authorities found eight-year-old Paul Bailly's body in the desolate hills of eastern Ventura County on March 23, 1990, not far from Greg's San Fernando Valley home. The eight-year-old's tiny frame, positioned beside a pair of handcuffs, was burned almost beyond recognition. The coroner, however, said Paul Bailly died of suffocation from the gag that was placed in his mouth before he was set on fire.

Greg was charged with sodomizing and killing eight-year-old Paul Bailly. It was one of the most brutal crimes ever in Ventura County history, rivaled only by Theodore Frank, who sexually tortured and killed two-year-old Amy Sue Seitz.

But there was one major difference: Theodore Frank was a man; Greg Smith was a child. Greg's mental age, according to mental health experts, was equivalent to that of an eight-year-old, the age of a child. The age of Mary Bailly's only son.

For the court's purposes, however, Greg only had to know the difference between right and wrong. Since he pleaded guilty to the crime, one would assume that Greg knew the difference. But did he know the consequences?

When I talked to Greg shortly before the trial began, it didn't seem as if he understood the reality of what was happening. Despite the gravity of the situation before him, Greg still had the indestructible mentality of a boy. He had no idea that this could really be the end for him, that he could die in jail, and the only question remaining then would be whether his death would be from natural causes or cyanide gas.

"I know I won't get the death penalty," Greg told me. "And if I do, I'll get it turned around...I know I won't die in the gas chamber."

In fact, Greg still thought that he was going to beat this thing, that he would somehow get out of jail someday. He didn't believe life in prison without the possibility of parole meant just that — no parole, not ever.

This was a dream to Greg, a dream that he said was controlled by God. He tried to get out of the dream by attempting suicide 10 times, but he couldn't slit his wrists because "I freak out at the sight of blood." God had saved him before, and God would save him again.

"I was a daredevil when I was little," he said. "I would do anything. I jumped from houses, I jumped from tree forts. I just wanted to know if I could do it."

Whether he could do it this time, however, was something even his attorneys questioned. All death penalty cases are tough. This one was a monster — an admission of guilt; a brutal murder; a dead little boy.

When the jury looked at Greg, they were going to see a killer, not a screwed-up kid. It was up to attorneys Jim Farley and Bill Wiksell to humanize Greg, make him a person again. And that would not be easy.

Jim and Bill didn't condone Greg's actions, not in the least. Bill told me that if he saw Greg coming near his house and his kids, he would pull out his shotgun and defend his family — without hesitation, without question. No one condoned Greg — how could they?

But Jim and Bill couldn't condone the government's desire, either. They wanted Greg punished, that's for sure, but they wanted the posse to take him alive.

So for months the drama of Greg Smith's fate was played out in Ventura County Superior Court. For months, a packed courtroom listened to the details of the crime, and to witnesses who said Greg was dangerous and should be executed. And there were those who testified that Greg's psychological state was that of a scared little boy, and that he didn't really understand the gravity of what he had done or the consequences he faced. Greg's mother took the stand, screaming, crying, begging for mercy for Greg Smith, the Human Being.

The prosecution spoke from the head, using graphs and charts and just the facts, ma'am, to persuade the jury to vote for death. The defense, however, spoke from the heart.

"He's a little boy," Bill told the jury. "That's all he is. Can little boys do bad things? Yes. And this one did. And he's going to spend the rest of his life in jail — if he's lucky.

"He's a child; he killed a child. Don't kill another one."

Greg's family rushed into the packed courtroom. Sherron Smith, Greg's mom, said they got the call from the bailiff at 4:15 p.m., and did between 80-85 mph from Beverly Hills to get here in time.

"It's going to be okay," she told her daughters. The family sat in the second row. Sherron put her hand over her heart as she tried to catch her breath. "This is scary," Sherron said.

Jim Farley walked in and sat down at the defense table, shaking his head.

"I think he knows," said Ellen, one of Greg's sisters.

"He doesn't know yet," answered Donna, a close family friend. Ellen pointed at her head with her index finger.

"Up here he knows," she said.

Donna got up and gave Jim a hug, and then sat back down with the family. "Bill and Jim did the best they could with what they had," she told me. "They are two wonderful men."

Donna sighed heavily. "Oh God."

Marvin Smith, the estranged father who abused Greg, both mentally and physically, was angry at all the media that had gathered to hear the verdict. Pointing at one photographer, he threatened to "knock him on his ass" if he tried to take a picture of the family.

Bill Wiksell joined Jim at the front table. Sherron wrung her hands, her face crumpled like a wad of paper. Greg's sisters, Ellen and Laura, held each other and took turns crying.

Waiting, waiting, waiting. The clock hit 6 p.m., and the president began his State of the Union address to all the nation — to everyone, that is, except those in Courtroom 22.

At 6:20 p.m., Mary Bailly walked in with her fiancee. No one in the Smith family picked their heads up to look.

Prosecutor Greg Totten motioned toward the bailiff.

"We're ready, Mark," he said.

The bailiff left the room. A few moments later he returned and called the courtroom to order. Judge Stephen Perrin assumed his seat on the bench.

"I do not know what the verdict is, nor do the counsel," he said. "Any outward displays of emotion (after the verdict is read) will be inappropriate."

The jury was brought in. Some of them looked at Greg, whose head was hung down to his navel. Most just looked down, or looked away. Greg was wearing a blue sweater that his mom gave him. Sherron was holding Laura's hand. It was her turn to cry.

Perrin addressed the stoic jurors.

"Has the jury reached a verdict?" he asked rhetorically.

The jury foreman, a tall, blonde woman, stood up and replied with a simple "yes".

Perrin: "Is it the unanimous opinion of all 12 jurors?"

Foreman: "Yes."

The foreman handed a slip of paper to the bailiff who gave it to the judge. Perrin glanced at the paper, and then read its contents aloud.

"We the jury in the above entitled cause fix the verdict at death."

Ellen cried first, then Laura, then Sherron. Marvin's eyes stayed closed, as they had been all through the trial, and all through Greg's life. Donna looked up and stared at the wall, where hung the inscription: "The Seal of the Great State of California."

The judge confirmed the verdict with each of the jurors. The foreman did her best to stop her tears, but she couldn't. It was supposed to be all over for them now, but it wasn't. You can't wipe away these kind of tears. These tears stay forever. These tears hold you accountable.

Greg cried, too. He cowered like a child and fell into Jim's burly arms — like the child that he was. Like a scared little boy lied to by his dreams.

Mary Bailly and the prosecutors, relieved and smiling, filed out to the waiting cameras and news people in the hallway. The Smith family stayed behind to be with Greg, if just for a few moments. As of now, every moment counted.

Donna hugged Jim and thanked him for trying. As the rest of the family came up to thank Jim and Bill, Greg was left alone at the table, his head buried in his hands.

As for me, I said my good-byes to the family as quickly as I could. I had intruded on their pain for months, and now it was time to leave them alone.

I wasn't much in the mood for talking, anyway. I only wanted to get out and get home before I had time to digest what had just happened. I almost made it, too. But there were too many reporters, and one of them stopped me before I could make my escape.

He wanted my reaction. He shoved a microphone toward my face and asked me what I thought. I stared at him for what seemed like an eternity.

I wanted to tell him all the reasons why this was wrong, even ludicrous. It would not save the state any money, would not prevent a murder, would not make us safer. It would not make our state, our society, our country a better place.

But I couldn't speak. I could barely think. All I could see was a dead little boy.

Was it Paul?

Was it Greg?

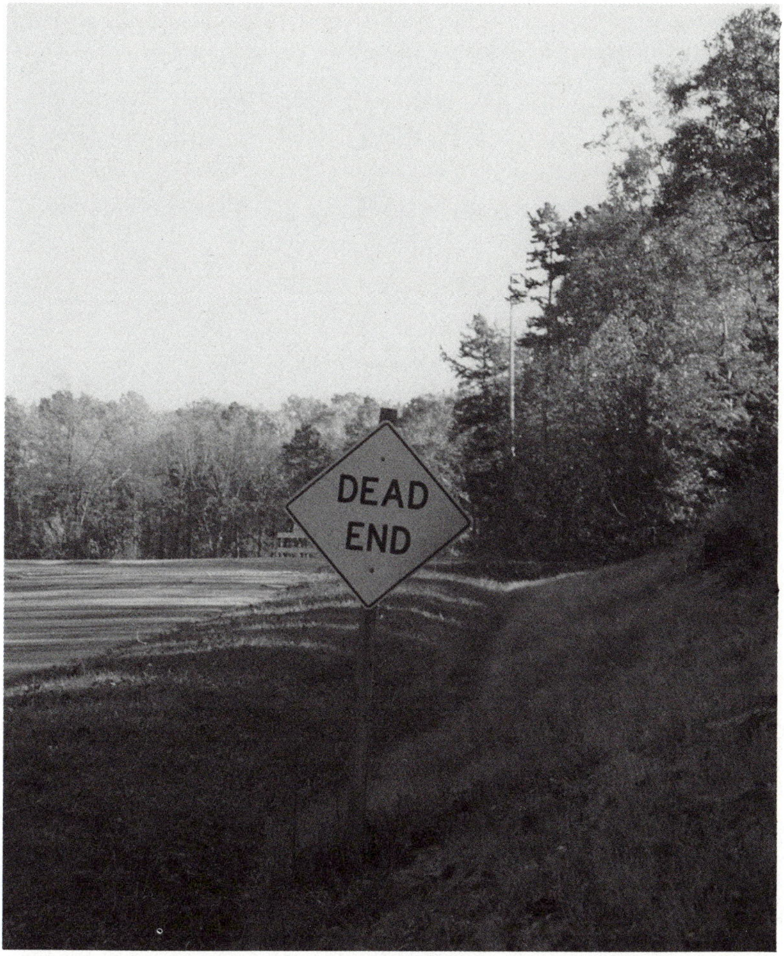

"*Entrance to Meckenburg Correctional Center, home of Virginia's Death Row.*"

BIDDLE PUBLISHING COMPANY

ORDER FORM

Please send _______ copies *Dead End* at $10.95 each ____________

Sales tax (Maine sales only) 6%, or $.65 ____________

Shipping, add $2.00 first book (or $4.00 for priority shipping); $1.00 each additional book ____________

TOTAL ____________

Send check payable to
Biddle Publishing Co.
PO Box 1305 #103   207-833-5016
Brunswick, ME 04011

Name ____

Address ____

____

Phone ____